WRITING FICTION:

CREATING THE FOURTH DIMENSION

by

C.J. HANNAH

PublishAmerica
Baltimore

First printing

At the specific preference of the author, PublishAmerica allowed this work to remain exactly as the author intended, verbatim, without editorial input.

ISBN: 1-4137-0801-2
PUBLISHED BY PUBLISHAMERICA, LLLP
www.publishamerica.com
Baltimore

Printed in the United States of America

WRITING FICTION:

CREATING THE FOURTH DIMENSION

by

C.J. HANNAH

TABLE OF CONTENTS

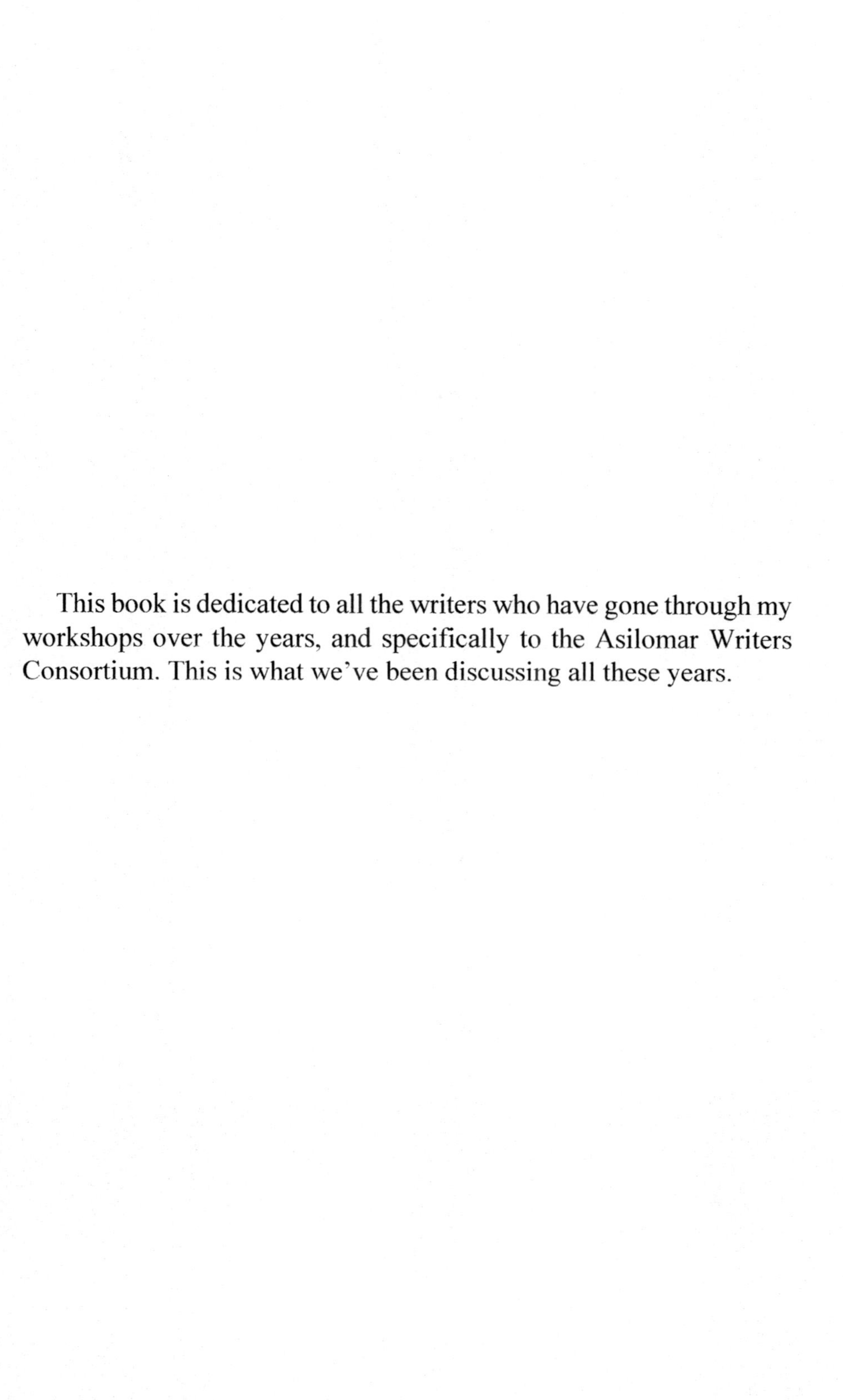

This book is dedicated to all the writers who have gone through my workshops over the years, and specifically to the Asilomar Writers Consortium. This is what we've been discussing all these years.

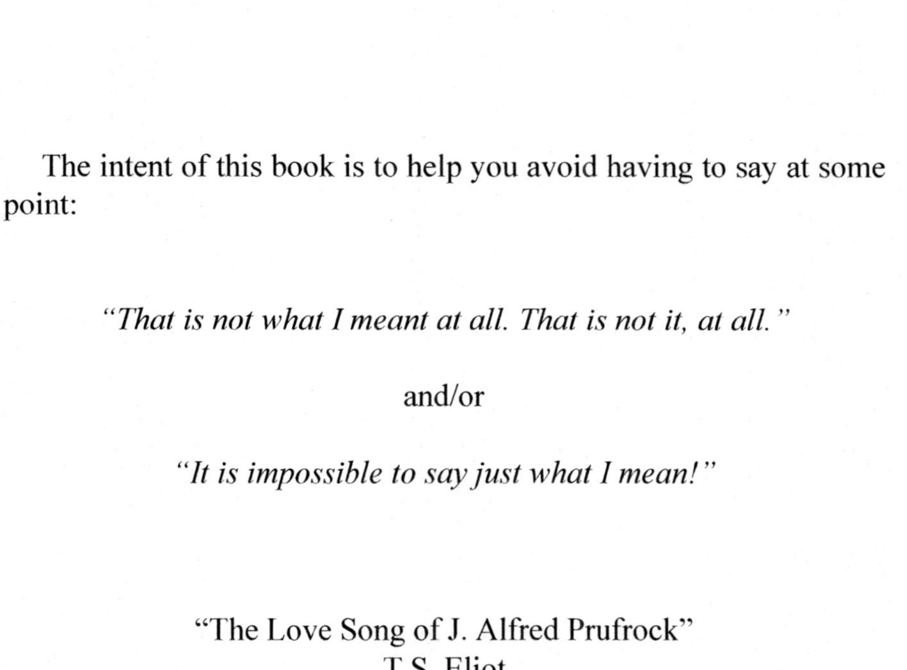

The intent of this book is to help you avoid having to say at some point:

"That is not what I meant at all. That is not it, at all."

and/or

"It is impossible to say just what I mean!"

"The Love Song of J. Alfred Prufrock"
T.S. Eliot

INTRODUCTION

"THERE ARE THREE RULES FOR WRITING [FICTION.] UNFORTUNATELY, NO ONE KNOWS WHAT THEY ARE."
W. Somerset Maugham

Your first question is probably, what makes this book on writing fiction the one you, a writer, would select over any others? This means 'credentials' and the best credentials I have are what other writers I've worked with say about me.

"Lots and lots of prolific and published writers have written books on writing (i.e., by writers for writers). It's not distinguishing. What distinguishes you is your incredible insight into the craft and your razor sharp ability to effectively express yourself in an understandable and implementable way. [Lauren Mummy]

"If it weren't for Jerry Hannah, I would never have had the courage to continue on the path leading me to my present career as a managing editor of two magazines and copy editor for a London Guardian/ Observer columnist. In early workshops, years ago, when I was a scared, nervous hopeful, I was mesmerized by Jerry's ability to "hear" commas, or where commas should be. He never missed slips in continuity or author intrusion or point of view changes. He possesses a phenomenal ear for the writing craft; he has inspired countless numbers of us who owe Jerry Hannah more than he will ever realize. I couldn't live without being able to writer for a living. Jerry Hannah gave me the foundation to DO that! I bless the day I first met this most gifted teacher." [Jerine P. Watson]

"After thirty years of writing television professionally, Jerry Hannah explained things to me in such a way about writing a novel, that concepts that've always eluded me suddenly are so clear that I can wrap my mind around them and not be afraid of doing it."[L. Brody]

"Jerry. If not for you this book would not have been. Love and gratitude," [Susan Vreeland] [Girl in Hyacinth Blue, one of the ten best novels of 1999 according to Publisher's Weekly, Christian Science Monitor and Small Booksellers Association, and Passion of Artemesia]

"Without Jerry to push, shove, shame, inspire and teach me, I would never have made it." [Sheila Finch] [winner of Compton Crook Aware for best first novel in science fiction and winner of the 1999 Nebula Award for her novella]

"We've been to many writers' conferences and classes all over the country and have found no one who compares with Jerry Hannah. Not only is his knowledge and skill in the craft of writing superb, his ability to communicate and teach his students is unsurpassed. Many of his students have gone on to have their novels published, movies made and even won esteemed writing awards." [Paul and Judy Bernstein]

"Jerry Hannah knows a great deal about the craft of writing, but more important, he has a rare gift for being able to communicate what he knows. He's been my teacher for over twenty years and any success as a writer that I've had or will have in the future, I owe him." [Rose Hamilton-Gottlieb]

"Jerry Hannah approaches writers with a unique blend of integrity, expertise and passion. In years of marveling at the effectiveness of his workshops, I've come to believe he just may be the world's best teacher." [J. J. Russ]

"Jerry Hannah may well be the reincarnation of Maxwell Perkins." [Barry Slater]

Three very good friends of mine, who are also writers, are giving me input about what should or shouldn't be in this book, and one question has come up from all three of them: Who is your audience? I've been thinking about that and this is basically what I've come up with: very, very serious writers, from beginners to professionals. I can't "write down" to anyone, but I try to be as clear as I can in explaining the various techniques. If someone is put off by the complexity of an idea, they probably won't want to use this book. The whole point is, writing fiction isn't easy and it isn't simple.

I'm proud of what I've had published, and I love to write, but, oddly enough, I value my teaching ability even more because of the many writers who have been in my workshops, now my friends, who have told me how much the workshops meant to them, how they gained insights into their own writing and moved ahead.

What I want this book to do is to make contact with as many writers as possible, and part of that contact is your ability, after you buy the book, to go to my website FictionSite.com and ask me questions or engage in discussions on writing. I envision a file where I can post your questions, statements, etc, and then respond to them. I'll keep updating the file and establish a library of questions-responses so you can access them. What I'm trying to do here, is meld electronic writing with traditional writing, which is something that very few books on writing fiction have done. In line with this, I also run a six week fiction workshops on line with FictionAdvice.com., so I'm fully into that electronic workshop as well.

My first goal with this book is to help you gain control of your writing, to know what's working or not, and how to find the solution.

We're going to establish a writer's vocabulary here, so that when we talk about writing we use a writer's vocabulary, not a reader's. . I'm going to include [I almost hate to use this phrase] writing exercises that will strengthen your abilities as a writer, help you overcome weaknesses in your writing, and basically turn you into a writer of marathon capabilities, i.e., in for the long run. I'm not going to use quotes from famous writers to demonstrate various techniques. I'm going to use my own material published and unpublished, to show you how I work, and in order to show you how to analyze your own work, I'll analyze mine.

I'm working under the assumption that since you're reading this book, or at least looking at it, at one level, you've already written something, or have something in mind you want to write and on another level, you're a writer who's been at it for quite some time. From beginning writers who have a character sketch, a place, an anecdote, something that sticks in their minds and demands that they do something with it, to the experienced writers who find themselves 'blocked' for some reason, this book is designed to help you.

A recent experience with these exercises will show their value even to a successful writer. A good friend of mine is an international best selling author, with two novels out in the past three years. She has been in my workshop for about 15 years, and I asked her to read a couple of sections of this book on writing. She did, and e-mailed me this note: "...went upstairs to bed and began reading your opening chapter about character. I thought, hm, good place to start, but then after I was reading for a while, I began to take notes in reference to Cedar Spirit, particularly regarding the sisters whom I didn't describe or differentiate in appearance. Then ideas came to me about their mannerisms, gestures, etc., and I tossed your chapter onto the bed and

went back downstairs, fired up the computer again, and added in the things I thought of, and have continued in that vein today. Which is to say...yes, Jerry, I guess it's working!!" A living e-mail testimonial!!!

I'm also going to show you how to set up a workshop that actually works, based on long experience. Wait, you say, what does this have to do with gaining control of my writing? Part of gaining, and keeping control, is to have feedback from other writers you can trust and depend upon. This is a survival technique but it is also a very, very difficult thing to find or establish.

In relation to that, a workshop I set up 27 years ago, is still going strong and we have some very successful writers who still participate. I've run the same type of workshop for the last 17 years, at the Southern California Writers Conference in San Diego and I was a workshop leader at the Santa Barbara Writer's Conference for the first seven years of that conference's existence. It was at that latter conference that I established the 'Pirate Workshop" which later led to the 'Rogue Workshop' in San Diego. I'm still refining my workshop, and I'll show you how the Asilomar Workshop Method works.

And finally, I'm going to include some of the Rose Notes, discussions on writing with writers on the internet and via e-mail. This section is basically me chatting with other writers about these questions that we all considered important to us as writers as well as points about various techniques. This is the kind of question-response we're going to be doing in the FictionSite.com file.

With all that said, I think there are a few more points to be covered, mostly to let you know what my attitudes are about writing. The most important is the idea that one genre is "better" than others, and that genre usually is called, "literary fiction." I recognize only one thing, all writers use the same techniques, thus, all genres are worthy of attention. I assume every writer wants to be as good as they possibly can be no matter what their chosen genre.

An interesting fringe benefit with this book, at least to me, is that it will also increase your reading enjoyment. I've always wondered why traditional literature classes weren't open to using the creative writing approach to teaching literature. I can't think of a better way to really get into an appreciation of literature than to approach it as a writer looking at what other writers do and how they do it. I've found that engineers, scientists and doctors enjoy my workshops because I show them the how of writing, which appeals to their love of concrete knowledge.

CHARACTERIZATION

The basic truth of writing good fiction is, character is story. This means the first thing to do is create a character that engages the reader's interest, which isn't as easy as it sounds. For example, there are at least 35 basic points of character that you, as an author, need to know. This is a bit intimidating, but there is nothing simple about creating a character. [the "begats" of Genesis notwithstanding]

Why is character the logical starting point? Primarily because everything else in the story flows out of character, i.e., the setting means nothing unless you have a character reacting to it or being acted upon by it. Dialog means nothing if it doesn't reveal character interaction, and most important of all, voice shapes the entire work, [much more about voice later] and without character there is no voice.

GENERAL CHARACTERIZATION CHART
name, nickname, gender, age, physical appearance
education, vocations, occupation,
status, [social, financial, marital
father-mother, family ethnicity, relatives, siblings, relationships
possessions, taste or preferences, pets, hobbies, recreation
obsessions, interests, beliefs, superstitions, attitudes,
politics

sexual history
character flaws and strengths, talents
ambitions, dreams,

The writer has to know all this about the character for the character to gain that four dimensional reality that fiction demands, and this includes knowing what the character lacks. For example, if the character has no political attitudes, beliefs, etc., that's an important thing to know, and if you ask why that character is apolitical, you begin to find another layer to their personality. Of course if you're writing about a child, the answer is self evident.

Another significant idea is that fiction is intensified reality, thus, your character has to reveal their complexity unlike someone in reality. This is another way of saying one of the most basic techniques in fiction is the use of hyperbole, deliberate exaggeration in order to make a point, which is why we read fiction.

To give you an idea of how complex the process of creating a character is, let me use a personal example. I'd been working on a novel, Ceremony of Innocence, for several months and it was 'okay' but there was something missing, something not quite there, and it seemed to be with the central character, whom I had named, arbitrarily, 'Paul.' Very boring, no reason for it, just a handy tag, and that was the problem. Then I asked myself, who his parents were, what were they doing when he was born, what interested them, etcetera, and before I realized it, I was doing a character chart on the parents, maybe not as detailed as Paul's, but detailed enough because they had a significant impact on him. It seems to me, that is also an authorial philosophy, i.e., parents have an impact on children that goes far beyond what we would think of as 'normal.'

First of all, I knew how old 'Paul' was, which meant I knew his birth date, which meant I should also know what was going on in the world at that time, and what was happening as he grew up. This led to knowing in some detail the place of his birth and subsequent experiences. I knew what 'Paul' believed in, basically the kind of person he was, but I hadn't considered where all this originated. At this point I developed his parents background. They were involved in the Viet Nam War protest movement and supported the United Farm Workers union under Cesar Chavez, various other liberal causes and out of that came 'Paul's' new name. At this point I began to insert these biographical details into the normal flow of the story. For example, in the first chapter:

We'd known each other since the third grade and became best friends when he told me he thought my name, Che, was cool. My left wing almost hippie parents, named me after Che Guevara, and I took a ration of shit about it. Still do.

And a few pages later:

My connection to the sheriff came from my, as he called them, 'hippie-liberal-do-gooder-bleeding-heart' parents who also knew Wapples. First hand. When word came back that they'd been killed in El Salvador by a School of the Americas trained death squad, Wapples said, 'The CIA finally did somethin' right.' He and I are old, old enemies.

The background of the parents is revealed as it becomes relevant to what Che is doing. So Paul Hadley became Che Hadley, and he had a very interesting background with his parents, which not only influenced him deeply, but opened up a whole new area of relationships for Che through his parents which in turn created a whole new subtext to the novel. The point here is that when I created the parents' background it was totally outside the scope of the novel and it's only mentioned briefly in the novel itself, but it shaped Che as a four dimensional character.

So, the central character's name became the most critical point in rewriting the novel, allowing me to go below the surface story and add depth and complexity. And that, my friends, is why character is important; it's the source of the fourth dimension.

Let me use a single point from the character chart to demonstrate how you should approach them. Take # 2 for example, the nickname. Nicknames can be either inclusive or exclusive, that is they can be rejection [exclusive] or acceptance, [inclusive], and it may not necessarily depend upon the kind of nickname. It's who gives the character that nickname. Peers are usually the source of nicknames and if you're being rejected, the exclusive nickname will have something personal and cruel in it, like Fats, or Slats.

However, if either one of those nicknames [Fats or Slats] came from an inclusive group, and were gently teasing, they change in impact. Also, if the character has moved away from the group that gave him the nickname, he or she wouldn't carry it with them if it was exclusive, but might if they were inclusive. If the character does carry the nickname to a new place, the source of the nickname is the character him or her self, which is an interesting and subtle point of the character's personality. The character's reaction to the nickname is critical, and it might not even be a factor in the work you're writing, but it is something the writer needs to know.

And think how sad it is for someone to have to give themselves a nickname. I recall a young man giving me his business card, and on it he had his name, and following it, 'also known as Duke.' That struck me as sad.

Also, if a character had no nickname, ever, that is also important, if the character is aware of that, or if the writer wants to make the reader aware of that. For example, this could come from the author to the reader, without the character's involvement: "Che never had a nickname, because his name was enough to exclude him from most of his fellow students, and to include him with the ones who were his friends. Che was politicized from birth."

You can even go to a simple name like "Jane," and point out to the reader [if you're in third person] that the parents really weren't all that involved with the child and simply named her because they had to have some sort of tag for her. "Jane" then becomes a significant rejection of her by her parents. She might not know that, but the author would, and can let the reader know that this kind of rejection is very important in understanding "Jane" later. And if "Jane" did know that, it becomes absolutely critical in understanding her. How did she find out that her parents didn't name her, but just 'tagged' her? From whom?

So you can see that a simple thing like a name or a nickname, takes on power and depth if the writer takes it seriously. As writers we need to be aware of how our culture works and how it shapes personalities, and a simple thing like a nickname demonstrates that awareness.

You need to approach each point of characterization that way; consider it in its entirety, its impact, its cultural background, etcetera. Play with them, but remember, writing is 90% hard work, and 10% inspiration, but the 10% is worth all the hard work.

The point of all this is that in order to get into your story, you need to create this character in all his/her complexity, get to know them better than you know yourself. I suggest going back to the General Characterization Chart and start making notes or writing passages that set your character up in your mind. Logically the first thing you should do is create a concrete image of the character, all the attributes mentioned in # 1, so that your character becomes a reality to you first. After that, it's more or less up to you to decide which of the attributes are more significant and develop them in descending order of importance. You may discover later, however, as you work with secondary and minor characters, or with setting, that something you thought was insignificant, becomes much more important due to the way the story developed. [this is part of that 10% inspiration that makes writing exciting]

As you develop your characters, you're going to have to put them into situations, [aka settings], which means you probably already have a place in mind that your character is going to be. Fine. Just do what comes naturally at the beginning, and don't worry about the complexities of setting, which we'll deal with later. The point to remember here is that reaction to setting is part of characterization. Later, when we come to setting, you'll find that developing your character here, is going to help you with setting later.

CROSS REFERENCE:
DEPTH IN CHARACTERS
RE: FEMALE CHARACTERS

For right now, just develop your character as a four dimensional human being. Let me explain. The three dimensions that we live in every day have to be there in the story for the character to live for the reader, but that fourth dimension is the one that the writer brings to the character, your understanding of her/him, your insights into their behavior, your reason for taking a close look at this person, and the degree of hyperbole you use with them.

I realize developing a character in this way is a very complex and time consuming, but if you use this technique, you're going to save yourself a lot of time rewriting. In a novel, I always go through this extensive characterization to a degree, usually when I'm working myself up to starting. Then once I'm writing it, I do use the check list to make certain I haven't left something out. It becomes almost second nature once you begin doing it.

In a short story, I usually have a character I've been thinking about for a while and I know the basics of his or her life: where they live, their education, background, attitudes, etc, but not in great detail. Once I begin the story, I write it through to the end, and along the way events or people will pop up that requires that I think about this aspect of the character's personality, but I don't stop there. I mark it, and then go on, because in my way of writing a short story for example, I have to get it all out in one sustained effort and then I'll go back and work on the marked areas. What I'm going for in the single sustained effort is story pace.

I don't think anyone can write a good story if they just "plug in" a character who has a name and a vague physical image. Most of us have much more specific characters in mind. All I'm doing with this technique is forcing you to think about what you know and should know about your character.

A "plug in character" usually means the plot line is more important than the character, and that will be evident in the story. Cliché characters are "plug in characters," like Tom Clancy's two dimensional central characters. [it's always fun to take a shot at a successful writer, isn't it?] "Plug in characters" are also a way of disguising autobiographical details, but the problem there is that the writer is usually unwilling to use the really interesting details about themselves for fear of revealing too much to the world. What happens there is that the character may have exterior details that are very good and very interesting, but interior details are lacking.

CROSS REFERENCE:
'WRITER AS CHARACTER'

Think about who your character is, and the more depth you give to them, the more interesting they're going to be to the reader, to say nothing about you, the writer. If a character is flat or two dimensional, the reader [assuming there ever will be a reader for a two dimensional character] is going to find it boring. Two dimensional characters only work as background, which is why plot driven novels usually have thin characterization, which leads me into the subject of:

CHARACTER TYPES IN FICTION.

I see them as basically in four groups and include them here because your central character is going to have to interact with these characters as you develop the central character's personality. Thus, you need to know how much emphasis should be given to these other characters in the story.

Central characters [this is the character we've been discussing]
Usually one in a short story, because you just don't have the time to develop more than one central character. In the novel you can have more than one central character, but you need to be very careful there. One thing to keep in mind is that it's a good idea to give the reader a

clear, concrete, physical image of the central character as soon as possible.

The central character should also be introduced very quickly in a short story, maybe within the first 150 words. If the central character is the controlling voice, [first person], then it begins from the first word, but if the author is the controlling voice, [third person], then it's within the first 150 words. When you decide to let your character tell the story, you have automatically opted for a 'story of character' because everything the reader knows comes from that character, and at the same time, reveals that character in depth. The only thing that may be missing in this type of story is a physical description of the narrator, unless you can work out a way to have him/her describe themselves without sounding egocentric or just dumb. An example of a 'quick character fix' is having a secondary character say to the narrator, "Man, you look just like Brad Pitt." There are other ways, such as using the description on a driver's license, etc, but the one thing you have to be certain of is that they fit within the natural flow of the story.

I have a character, Hoover, who narrates a series of stories called The Holy City Zoo. The thing is, he sounds at first like a distant, third person narrator, one who is observing the scene but not in it, but very quickly the reader realizes he is in the scene because other characters are talking to him and he replies. The difference there is that when he speaks, he never tags his own line, but he does for everyone else. This means that he is always part of the action in order to tell us about it, but he takes on the personality of a distant observer, with an attitude. For example, from The Holy City Zoo, The Little Animals of God Pet Cemetery and Shrine:

Pussytoes got custody of the stuffed, fourteen foot, py-thon with the two headed calf stuck up on the front of it when Shanahan moved down to Dismal Seepage and opened up a Sinclair gas station there. Once he was gone, Pussytoes sorta funked out and took to sittin' in the Holy City Bar and Mineral Water Baths, drinkin' water glasses of Old Crow, lookin' like a carnival kewpie doll going bad, slow.

We all tried to cheer her up but it wasn't no use. She just sat there in the bar, paintin' B. B. King's face on one side of these flat river rocks and Baby Jesus on the other, sellin' them to tourists as Rocks of Ages. Believe that was her Blues Period.

In the last paragraph of the example, the narrator lets the reader know that he is a part of this scene by using "We." An example of third person distant narration is from my novel, Ceremony of Innocence: Mattathias knew who he was, a deep awareness, as much a part of him as his bones, the marrow of his bones, the confidence, self assurance of the dominating class:

his people on the North American Continent for over three hundred years, his Highland Scot ancestors arriving in Nova Scotia in 1650,

the Highland clans being massacred in the Old Country,

arriving here as outlaws, exiles, moving West across the Continent, pushing farther and deeper into the beautiful vastness of the frontier, sometimes alone, sometimes marrying Indian women,

sometimes waiting for another Highland refugee to arrive,

until in the nuclear half of the twentieth century, he, Mattathias Robertson,

the sixth generation, stood on the final Western edge of the continent,

turned,

looked back toward the Rocky Mountains and

made his stand.

The structure is a little unusual but the point here is that what makes it third person is the use of the proper name "Mattathias" followed by a more formalized stream of consciousness. If I had used the personal pronoun 'he' then it would be set up for a possible close voice narrator, that is the character thinking rather than the narrative voice summarizing, and this would have meant a change in the style of the stream of consciousness section, which would have made it more emotional but much less understandable. I decided to go for the intellect here rather than the heart, that is, I had the narrative voice tell the reader these things rather than have the character recall them in his own words.

Secondary characters: The number here depends upon how complex the plot line is and the nature of the central character. Again, in a short story, you'll probably have only one because the focus of a short story is very tight, which means detailed and quick. The secondary character is named, has a recognizable style of speaking, and is clearly described to the reader. Their importance is determined by their relationship with the central character, and one of the things a secondary character can do that is critical is to give information to the reader that the central character may not have. This requires a shift in focus.

CROSS REFERENCE:
POINT OF VIEW SHIFTS

Shifting point of view, also called shifting the focus character, is a more complex use of a secondary character, moving away from the central character and letting the reader see a setting in which the central character normally wouldn't be found. For example, in my novel Ceremony of Innocence, I shift to a secondary character, Dillard Tucker, the owner of a bar and use him as the focus character for the entire chapter. I structured this chapter to move from general to specific, i.e., showing first what Dillard sees every day but is unaware of, to specific details of which he is aware.

The early morning regulars of The Track sit hunched and mute over their boilermakers, but not silent. Snuffling, wheezing, coughing phlegm up out of their chest and throats. Spitting with indifference into the lard buckets placed along the bar rail at their feet. Old men with stained, faded baseball caps pulled low over their eyes, lifted glasses of beer with slow delicacy. Stretching the drink as far as possible. Needing to gulp it down but afraid their money will run out, leave them nothing to drink. No place to go. No one to sit next to. Their hands are scarred, fingertips thick, broken nails permanently dark with grease, dirt, a lifetime of hard work at low pay. The muscles in their arms and shoulders gone slack, backs permanently hunched from years of physical labor. They squint down at the bar top. Unwilling to face each other in the mirror of the back bar. Each man knows he still looks good, could still put in a day's work. But his friends have gone to hell. Turned into old, broken down wrecks. Not all are old. Young men in yellow and orange hard hats, hunch over the first drink of the day. The hair of the dog before work. Shoulder to shoulder with the old men. Unaware they are sitting next to themselves in fifteen or twenty years. Still believing they will always be young, and strong, and working.

Dillard Tucker knows this, sees it, understands it. But in no articulate way. He has watched the transformation. Observed it over the years behind the bar in The Track, but only thinks of it as a ceaseless flow of customers who never seem to change.

Then the details that Dillard is aware of: He picked another powdered sugar donut out of the now half empty box on the bar. Bit off half of it. Washed it down with a mouthful of lukewarm coffee. The front door opened. A flash of sunlight and a puff of cool morning air. The door quickly closed. No one at the bar looked up. Dillard, standing at the far end of the bar away from the door, reached for another donut. Watched the new customer move silently to a middle stool. Dillard paused, donut in one hand, coffee cup in the other. Staring. That's the sonofabitch was talking to Wayne the other day. Wonder what he's up to. He finished the donut in two bites, two gulps of coffee, wiped his mouth with the back of his hand. And moved deliberately down the bar to the new customer. Stopped in front of him. Waited silently.

Minor characters: These characters will be quickly described, maybe with a particular physical trait to set them apart, like "A short man with a hawk-like nose, who twitched nervously." The reader is able to see them quickly, but they may or may not have names. They can speak, and may have an exchange with the central or secondary character. Usually they're used to move the plot along, introduce a complication or something like that. It's not necessary to go into any extensive detail of their background but they do need a physical presence.

A point I need to make here is that in this collection, 'The Holy City Zoo' minor characters in one story may become secondary characters in another, because the entire collection is centered around these citizens of Holy City. The central character is, throughout all the stories, Hoover, the narrative voice. What happens in each story is that the focus character changes, that is the character around whom the action is centered, the character Hoover focuses on.

Background characters: These are characters used to fill out a scene and have no more significance than a bush or a tree. They're just used to give the scene depth, and many times used to show how aware the central character is of the scene. For example: "Three men in worn black suits, each carrying a scarred brown briefcase, and a young woman in a red dress, stood at the bus stop." Just background, but it's a detail that could make the scene come alive.

Here is an exercise in which you can use your reading talents to further your understanding of characterization. Select a favorite short story and do the following:

5 MINUTES:

LIST AS MANY CHARACTERISTICS OF THE CENTRAL CHARACTER'S PERSONALITY AS YOU CAN.

GIVE A QUICK REFERENCE TO WHERE IN THE STORY YOU SAW THIS

5 MINUTES:

DO THE SAME FOR THE SECONDARY CHARACTER

REFINE YOUR LISTS BY SEPARATING THE QUALITIES INTO POSITIVE/NEGATIVE

REFINE THAT LIST BY COMBINING SIMILAR QUALITIES

UNDER A GENERAL HEADING LIKE PREJUDICES OR HABITS.

WRITE A BRIEF, BUT ACCURATE, EVALUATION OF BOTH CHARACTERS

The idea of the timed responses in # 1 and #2 is to demonstrate how clearly and quickly the character was put in your mind by the author. In #3. #4, #5, and #6 you're considering the total impact of the characterization but now in some detail that explains why you reacted to these characters the way you did. As a writer, you're asking, "How did the author do that?"

CHARACTER'S BIOGRAPHY: Now you need to write your character's biography, not a story, but the biography of this person who exists in your fictional world. Admittedly we're reversing the traditional order of creation a little, starting with human beings first, then creating the world, but in our approach the character is the story, not the setting, so that's where we begin.

You can use a character you've already used in a story, or create a new one, but if you use an already existing character, remember that you're now developing him or her more fully. Here's what you should do, using your authorial voice:

summarize your character's early life, childhood through adolescence, hitting the significant points more strongly. You can begin earlier than childhood and end later than adolescence if you want, but you want to end the biography at the point you pick them up in the story you're writing. The reason for this is so that there will still be a process of discovery for you which lends freshness to the work, to say nothing of fun for you as you discover new things about your character.

describe the physical environment during those formative years.

describe relationships with his/her parents, siblings if any and other relatives as well.

describe relationship with a best friend, if any, and peers.

describe relationship with a pet or favorite toy or object.

describe two significant events in childhood that effected him/her in some basic way. It doesn't have to be traumatic, just very influential.

describe their educational experience

describe their parents, including physical characteristics, background, socio-economic status, education, general life style, dominant parent, major attitudes, etc.

describe any intimate relationships, including sexual

Check the characterization chart for any unusual details in his/her background and explain how/why they came about

describe your character's dreams and hopes, fears and ambitions

have your character tell you about some recent experience that changed him/her in some way. This should have nothing to do with the story you're going to write because you want those events to be fresh, not recycled. Be sure to think of how this character talks, their speech patterns [syntax] and rhythms, their vocabulary, etc.

CROSS REFERENCE:
FIRST PERSON P.O.V. GRAPHIC

What you're probably going to find here is that as you're developing anecdotes about your character, some of them will become so detailed you immediately realize they are significant, while others will simply remain enriching anecdotes. This is that wonderful process of discovery that makes writing fun.

A word of reassurance here; as you write these exercises, you're using what you already know consciously or unconsciously about writing techniques, and as you go on through the various techniques, you're going to understand what you didn't know and correct that, or you're going to realize there were techniques that you did know and used well. What this means is that you're going to understand that rewriting is the process of true creativity, and when you being to do that, you're showing yourself as a serious writer.

CROSS REFERENCE
GOOD VS OTHER WRITING

POINT OF VIEW

Point of view [p.o.v.] is equal in importance to characterization. They are inextricably intertwined and it's impossible to write anything unless you understand the two basic points of view, first and third. Point of view simply means, who is telling the story, the author, a narrator or a character.

At its most simplistic, **first person** is the "I" point of view, the character in the story narrating it. Here is a basic first person p.o.v. from my story, "No Return Address:"

I have come to hate picking up my mail. I peek in through the tiny window in the mail box to see if there's a post card there, not wanting to open the box if there is, yet I always do. The worst part is not being able to answer him. He never puts on a return address. Sometimes the only way I can tell where he is, is by the postmark and sometimes they're unreadable. Today I see no card, just junk mail catalogues, bills and a letter from my sister. I feel a strange sense of relief. I open the box, pull out the mail and the card falls on the floor. I stare at it.

Third person is the "he, "she," or the name of the character, like "Matt." Here the narrator of the story is outside the story, not a participant. For example, from my short story "Joining the Dinosaurs:"

Matt sat in the shade of a wind carved, sandstone cave, his rifle propped against one shoulder, the freshly killed rabbits on the rough floor next to him. Several hundred yards below him and to the northeast, Uncle Vic was laboring up a mica flaked hogback, heading toward the abandoned coal mine. Matt knew why he was going there. The dinosaur track his grandfather found. Somehow or other Uncle Vic had heard about it, and now he was going up there to figure out a way to get it out of the mine so he could sell it. The sonofabitch.

In the previous example, the third person voice is set up by the use of the name "Matt," and every time the author uses the character's name, it is a third person reference. The syntax, the more distant, objective tone of the descriptions, are also indicative of the third person voice. The phrase "his grandfather" is also third person narration, but if you wanted it in the character's voice you would simply use "Grandfather" and the capitalization along with the dropping of the pronoun "his" would indicate a shift to the character's voice.

When you began to develop your character's biography, I forced a point of view on you. At first it was the third person, you using the authorial voice, the third person narrative voice, then in number 12, I forced you to use the first person point of view, the character's voice. In both cases, due to the kind of material you were writing, several more things about the point of view were forced on you. For example, when you were using the authorial/narrative voice, you were forced to be objective, observational, accurate. When you shifted to the character's voice, you were forced to be subjective and emotional. If your character chart was detailed enough, you would know how the character spoke, syntax, vocabulary, tone, etc. If you didn't know, you need to go back and fill in that part of the characterization.

What you were doing in #12 [first person], shifting to the character's voice, was most likely more by instinct and because of your reading. As a writer you have to make conscious choices about which point of view you're going to use, why and how to shift back and forth between the two voices, that is the distant voice and the close voice, in both points of view. Mastering point of view sounds easy on the surface, but there is much more to it than a simple proper noun-pronoun choice.

First And Third Person Point of View

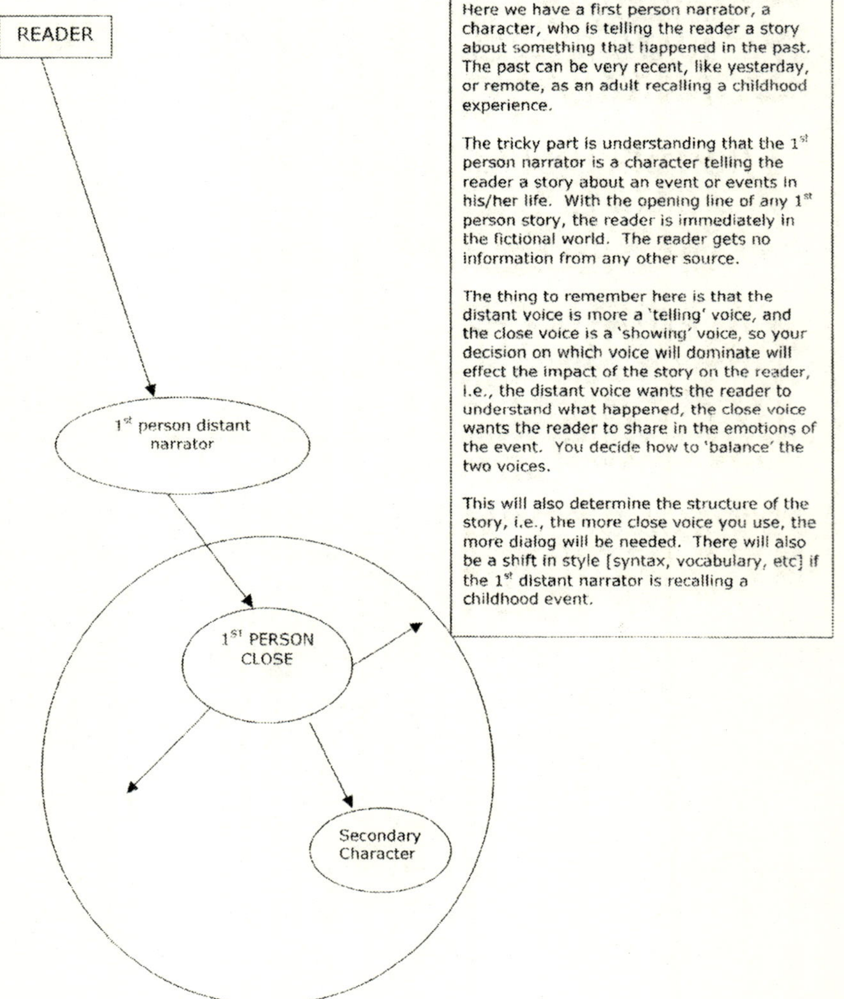

WHOSE STORY IS THIS ANYWAY?

First Person Point of View: This is the "I" point of view, and although it seems fairly simple on the surface, there is a little more to it. There are actually two voices in the first person:

A **distant voice**, the voice recalling the events of the story after they've already happened. For example, an adult recalling a childhood experience.

This distant voice knows how it all turned out and is in control of the events. Nothing can surprise this voice because it is in control of the events. The style here is usually very smooth, flowing, deliberate. The first person distant voice is, in effect, the style of the character rather than of the author. Passive constructions are used, i.e., "The cow was hit by the road grader," rather than the active voice, "The road grader hit the cow." The syntax in this voice will likely be more complex because the character is consciously recalling events. This voice will usually be the one to use metaphors and similes.

CROSS REFERENCE
FIGURATIVE LANGUAGE

An example of first person distant voice comes from my short story, "Billy Beauchamp:"

And every time I think of the hard rock mine at Liberty, I get this picture in my head of Billy Beauchamp, standing in the concrete shaft house, waiting for the bucket to take us down into the mine. The swing shift's standing there hunched up inside themselves, smoking and watching the bucket cable whine away, dropping a load of miners a couple of thousand feet underground to number twenty-five stope. It's cold in the shaft-house, mostly because of the wind blowing up out of the shaft, like the mine was breathing. Billy's standing off alone, his head tilted back, looking up toward the four windows at the top of the shaft house where the bucket cable winds around a big pulley. The sun's coming in through of one the windows, shining down on Billy, who keeps moving with the light, like he can't get enough. Just staring up at that window like he was never going to see the sun again. He was eighteen then. Never saw nineteen.

A **close voice**, the voice of the character as s/he goes through the experience and is surprised by the events because this voice has no idea of how things are going to turn out. It is immediate and active. More prompted by the emotion of the moment.

The 'style' of the close voice is more personal, vernacular, reflecting personality more than accuracy. For example, the close voice [character] might drop 'ing' endings or have a repetitive phrase they use unconsciously, like "Okay." Both the distant and the close voices are biased points of view, i.e., the character warps reality according to his or her own view of the world. This again is a tricky bit, i.e., in the distant voice the character is at least attempting to maintain some objectivity about the events, but in the close voice there is no attempt to do that.

Basically, the close voice is the voice of action, while the distant voice is the voice of thought, of deliberation. If you want your reader to have more of an intellectual reaction, to be more contemplative or thoughtful, you go to the distant voice. If you want your reader to react emotionally to the story, you go with the close voice. You're going to use both voices in any first person story, it's just the emphasis you want to give the story that tells you which voice you want to dominate. The only time you would use only first person close, would be in a present tense story in which the action is happening as the story goes on. The usual verb tense for fiction is past tense, for a lot of reasons the most common being that is the tense to which readers are most adjusted.

Another way of describing the difference between the distant and close voices is this; close is showing, distant is telling. Showing is dramatic and telling is intellectual, but this is an oversimplification. The distant voice can describe a scene, using all five senses to create a vivid image in the reader's mind, and that description, because it is in the first distant voice, would have an emotional content to it, but it's still distant because it's a scene being recalled, not one being experienced in the moment.

Here's the first person close voice from my short story "Pay Back:"

From my table in the rear of the cafe I can see my target up near the front, seated at a small round table, drinking a cup of espresso. His brown tweed hacking jacket and white on white silk shirt seems an affectation in this place, yet knowing Lester as I do, I know the affectation is as much the cafe, the small white cup of espresso and the Italian opera on the juke box. Lester's life has been an affectation since we were nine years old, when he painted the name HELLCAT on his Flexible Flyer sled, dipped snuff, and told dirty jokes he didn't understand.

When you decide to let your character tell the story, [first person] you have automatically opted for a 'story of character' because everything the reader knows comes from that character, and at the same time, reveals that character in depth. The only thing that may be missing in this type of story is a physical description of the narrator unless you can work out a way to have him/her describe themselves without sounding egocentric or just dumb. An example of pure first person distant narrative paragraph from my collection of short stories, The Holy City Zoo:

Well sir, me an' Old Ralph and Woody was settin' on a old wood bench under the green dinosaur sign at the Sin-clair station when Shanahan Poe, our Foundlin' Father, as Old Ralph likes to call him, first showed up in his red, half ton, Diamond-T truck loaded with abalone shells, and sittin' right there next to him, covered with brown road dust, was Francealene Madigal Baker, ex-flower child, ex-commune organic vegetable farmer, ex-channeler for some dead Druid or other, her eyes squintin', her mouth pooched in a pout, huggin' herself like she was about to bust out screamin'. Not a happy hippie.

The use of vernacular like hyphenating 'Sin-clair ' to imply a specific pronunciation or the phrase, 'pooched in a pout," the dropping of the 'g'' in 'ing' endings, and in the opening line, the use of "me an' old Ralph and Woody," all indicate a first person narrator, but his attitude is one of a distant third person narrator. At the end of the story, the reader realizes [hopefully] that the narrator has revealed more about himself than anyone else in the story because it's his take on his world. By the way, the only thing the reader never knows about Hoover, is what he looks like.

I deliberately did this for various reasons, but the most significant is that I want the reader to create Hoover physically from all that they know about him, thus the reader creates an acceptable physical image of the narrator for themselves.

This can be a subtle and very effective point of view, but an unusual first person narrator can cause you problems with readers. For example, in The Holy City Zoo I found it sometimes difficult to get readers [mostly editors and agents] to accept this narrator's view of his world as valid because he sounds too "redneck." Readers are accustomed to having a standard English, educated, middle class narrator, like an adult Tom Sawyer, but I decided to go for 'Huckleberry Finn's' great, great, great grandson. It's important to remember that a first person narrator can alienate the readers, so s/he must be set up very carefully.

The **first person close voice**, is the same character who narrates in the distant voice, but now the character is participating in the action rather than observing it. For example, from my short story, "Shooting versus Killing:"

"Now, Mattathias, you always keep me in sight. Never get too far ahead or behind your partner. Keep on line with me."

"Yes sir."

"And don't shoot until you know what you're shooting at."

"Yes sir."

"Okay, son, let's go get 'em."

I walk just like Father. Stalking he calls it. I hold my gun at 'port arms.' Ready to shoot. Anything. I pretend the enemy is somewhere out there in front of us. Hiding in the sage brush. Just me and Father. Alone. Against THEM.

In this particular example, I shift to present tense verbs to impart the feeling of immediacy. With that brief explanation of first person point of view you're ready to work with it. [Assuming things is what makes teaching the mental equivalent of running through a mine field, wearing oversized clown shoes.]

EXERCISES FOR FIRST PERSON POINT OF VIEW

We're still working on getting to know this character and one of the most effective ways to do that is to use their voice [first person] to reveal more about their life. Now write the following short pieces in first person to both reveal your character and to begin to develop their own voice, style, syntax, and vocabulary. You're already aware that speech rhythms and patterns mark individuality and reveal more about us than we realize, but now as a writer you must consciously create those in your character. Notice I said 'in' your character, not 'for.' Don't make them puppets, make them live.

Write about 500 words for each of the following:

In the first person distant voice, have the character describe a significant person from childhood.

For example, from my short-short entitled 'The Queen of Cedar Mesa:'

I knew her well, saw her every Saturday, she always spoke nicely to me, smiling, and she smelled like Mrs. Bardell's rose garden. Her name was Rita Stillwater. She lived alone on Cedar Mesa with two blue tick hounds and a flock of chickens from which she brought brown eggs to Eckert's Grocery each Saturday, trading for sugar and flour to make cakes and cookies. She traded hand thrown pottery at Jackish's Store for bolts of cloth, spools of thread, buttons to make her dresses which gave her the name, The Queen of Cedar Mesa, frocks she called them, long, floating diaphanous creations of blue and peach and lemon yellow, worn with large Spanish hoop earrings, and Navajo bracelets of hammered silver, soft, hand-sewn slippers of elkskin and a huge, white straw hat to shade her fair, pale skin, a legacy of her thick red hair tumbling over her shoulders.

In the first person distant voice, have the character describe in detail one significant event from the their life. [passive recalling]

For example, from my short story, "The Mortality of Kodak Moments:"

A small old man, behind a tall black iron gate, hands gripping round bars, a yellow plaid, wool hat, ear flaps pulled down and tied under his chin, peers out at passersby. Safety pinned on the hat's crown, a shaky hand drawn sign in black crayon:

LITTLE BOY BLUE

TRULY LOST

I remember him vividly.

I remember most especially a vague, uneasy sense of recognition.

I buy photographs in junk stores. Images crammed into shoe boxes marked with red crayon, 25 cents each. Photos taken in the early 1900s when cameras were unusual, special. People just beginning to record themselves. Now their beloved images are stacked in an old Florsheim shoe box in Mother Maybelle's Memorabilia. Sold for a quarter each. Low value in an over recorded age.

In the first person close voice, have the character describe the same character as in #1 [same scene, active, involved]

Lester said I was crazy the way I always watched for her, the Queen of Cedar Mesa. She had this wire basket she carried brown eggs in only now it was empty because she'd traded to Mr. Eckert for stuff to make cakes and cookies. Sometimes she had some with her and she always gave me one. Lester never got any. When she got closer she smelled like Mrs. Bardell's rose garden. Her real name was Rita Stillwagon. She lived up on Cedar Mesa, all alone. Well, not all alone, she had two blue tick hounds and some chickens. And she wore these neat dresses, frocks she called them. All peachy and lemony colored. And she had these big silver earrings, and lots of Indian bracelets. And real deer skin moccasins.

In the first person close voice, have the character relate the same event in #2 in the first person close and distant voice have the character relate another significant event in their life. Make the close voice dominate.

Keep in mind in each of these pieces that there could be a change in the vocabulary, attitudes, etcetera. between the distant and close voices, depending upon how far back in the character's life you go for the memory. For example, if the distant voice is recalling the event, s/he knows how it turned out and they can be more objective about it. However if the close voice is experiencing the event, the tone will probably be more emotional about the event as it happens.

Third Person Point of View: Everything said about the close and distant voices in first person, holds true in the third person with one major exception; the distant third person voice is not a character in the story. It is a voice outside the story but a voice that knows everything going on in the story. It has also been called omniscient, the all seeing voice, the author's voice. This voice has the freedom to move anywhere, at any time, including into the minds of all the characters, and is not restricted in any way. This third distant voice should also be separated from the close voice(s) of the characters, by style, syntax, vocabulary, etc. The third distant style is normally one of control, of deliberation or preciseness, of intellectual interest and it is objective. You'll notice I said 'normally' because there are uses of this voice that differ. The thing you need to do is master the basic form first, then begin to experiment. Here's an example of third person distant voice:

Che hiked up the canyon, careful not to step into any prickly pear cactus patches and constantly looking for any rattlers out sunning themselves in the early morning sun. About two hundred yards away, on the south wall of the canyon was a huge redstone overhang stained black from ancient fires, and just over the tops of the pinon trees the crumbling edge of an adobe wall were visible. An Anasazi ruin.

The opening word, "Che" sets up the distant voice, and from that point on the reader gets nothing but visual reporting in the distant voice which is one characteristic of the distant voice here. Also there are no emotions, no reactions, so it remains distant. Ideally there should be a clear difference between the third close and distant voices, which means your central characters should not sound like the third distant voice. They should have a distinct style of their own that is immediately recognizable in terms of syntax, vocabulary, awareness, or in the view they have of the events, i.e., a distant voice will comment and describe events objectively but won't participate in them. For example, here's the opening paragraph from Ceremony of Innocence that shifts from distant to close voice:

Mattathias hesitated just outside the door to Jack Riley's Seattle apartment, found himself breathing a little too rapidly as if he was about to confront someone he knew was hostile. But that wasn't it. Admit it. What it was, was his growing reluctance to go out again at Jack's command. Put himself on the line. Begin one more fight they would eventually lose. No. That he would eventually lose. That about summed it up lately. No longer 'the cause.' He'd lost what Jack claimed was the basic element of a true believer; fanaticism.

The opening phrase, "Mattathias hesitated…" is third distant voice due to the use of his name, but in the next line, "But that wasn't it." the syntax shifts to an abrupt style, more conversational, and in the next line, "Admit it." there is a distinct syntactical shift to the character's voice, and from that point on it's in close voice. The sentence structure here makes the difference, i.e., the jump from a complex syntax to abrupt syntax, which continues. The tension in the abrupt lines from that point on, comes from the character. I want to stress the idea of tension here for a moment. Tension in the distant voice is created in the reader through the action in the story, and that tension can be implied with a subtle shift in syntax from normal or complex to very abrupt. Tension in the characters comes from the close voice, their reactions to the events, etc around them. I think the simplest way I can put that is that tension in the reader is manipulation by the distant voice; tension in the character is caused by events, other characters, etc. in the story.

CROSS REFERENCE:
ESTABLISHING RHYTHMS

The same holds true here in terms of using both distant and close voices to elicit a particular reaction from the readers: **Distant voice** = objective, understanding, insightful, literate, creative, always apart from the action. **Close voice** = emotional, subjective, real, flawed, always involved in the action

The advantage of the third distant voice is its ability to fill in those details of the world of the characters, that are beyond the capabilities of the characters.

For example, if you have a character who is very unaware of his/her surroundings, in the third person, the distant voice can fill in the settings for the reader. This would be impossible if the character remained unaware in both the distant and the close voice. That's why in stories where a character is involved in intense action, you shift to the distant voice to describe the setting, because in the close voice it's simply not believable that a character under that much emotional or physical stress would notice the setting. When you are writing an intense action scene, you have to decide on what reaction you want your reader to have, i.e., do you want them to be able to see it and understand it, [distant voice] or do you want them to feel it, [close voice]? For example, I decided I wanted the reader to understand and see the action vividly rather than experience it in my short story "The Shadow Witness:"

Lester leaped at him, hit him in the face. The Indian kid fell back, stunned, unprepared. Lester crowded closer, hit him in the stomach, in the face, left hand alternating with right, the Indian kid's head slewed around, his face grotesquely mashed, his body flung out of control, and the crowd screamed,

"Get him Lester, kill him Lester!"

Girls hid their faces behind spread fingers. Boys' faces melted, slack with fearful ecstasy. Bellowing at the violence not directed at them.

A more complex example of both close and distant voice, shifting and refocusing is in this excerpt from The Ghostdancers, Book in which a minor character, Weaver, is attacked by Taggert, with a psi-weapon. The first paragraph, first line "The door to the dormitory…" is in distant voice, then it shifts to a transition line which helps refocus the voice, "Taggert snorted" and then it goes into Taggert's voice with, "Like he didn't…" Then in the italicized paragraph the reader 'see's what Taggert 'sees' in Weaver's mind, which is also close voice. The line leading into the italicized paragraph, 'He focused on Weaver…' is the distant voice,

The door to the dormitory opened and Weaver swaggered in, grinning at everyone as he smoothed his hair back with long sweeps of both hands. Taggert snorted. Like he didn't know nothin'. Like that fucken Weaver hadn't gone into his footlocker and stole his deck of girlie cards and his cigarettes. He hated that kinky haired black sonofa…He focused on Weaver, imagined boring a hole in his head, going inside…

maggots…great white masses of fat maggots writhing on a black plate…fingers like swollen white sausages reaching out to them…plucking them up…dropping them into a mouth, the lips thick, fleshy, purple and red…thick yellow juice squirted out from between twisted green stained teeth…

Taggert shut the image down quickly, sickened by it. [distant voice to close voice] What kinda punk had shit like that in his head? Well, he'd just go in quick, like a, a, flame thrower. Yeah, a flame thrower, just burn him out.

At this point I have to shift back to the distant voice in order to tell what Taggert is doing, but which he would be unaware of because he's involved in a murderous attack and basically out of control due to the drug he's been given.

Taggert stared hard at Weaver focusing totally on him. Everything around Taggert dimmed, disappeared. He could feel the power rising up in him. He could feel his eyes widen. Images of fire, yellow, orange, blue poured from him in a solid beam like a flashlight in a pitch black cave…

Weaver shrieked, grabbed his head with both hands, his mouth twisted open wide as the scream grew, he stumbled across the room…

Taggert backed off a little, wanting Weaver to feel it more, to have to live with the pain for a little longer…

The scream died into a whining, moaning cry of pain. Weaver fell to his knees, both hands still grasping his head as if trying to hold something in, long strings of spittle drooled down from his mouth and he rocked back and forth like a praying man. A strong, sickening odor filled the room as Weaver lost control of his sphincter.

Taggert's lips curled back in disgust. [shift to close here] Just like a nigger. [and back to distant] He focused again, pouring every bit of his power into Weaver again and he stiffened, his eyes wide, distended, his mouth stretched grotesquely open, so wide it seemed he would tear his face apart, but there was no sound, nothing. He grew rigid, then fell forward, hands still grasping his head.

In this last paragraph the one line of close voice, "Just like a nigger," and the return to the distant voice was done because my decision here was that it was more important for the reader to vividly see what Taggert was doing, rather than to 'see' it through Taggert, which would have been incoherent.

Also, there are moments in a story when a character is just moving through a place with no conscious thought of what the setting is, so the distant voice steps in and shows the reader what the character is seeing on a subconscious level. For example from my short story, "An Image of Truth":

Walking along the beach, dainty steps across the slick black stones exposed by the low tide, avoiding the globules of oil, the scum discharged by a passing tanker, coming across a sea bird, a parody of a sea bird, black and stiff with oil, lying on a small crescent of sand between two huge boulders, he sits down beside the bird, tucking his feet in under him, the book-pack cradled in his lap, staring at the oily corpse, wondering why he was there and if there was room in his book for the bird.

The idea here is that this is what the character sees without consciously registering it, something we do every day with familiar scenes. However, if the character does actively notice the setting, the setting becomes much more significant in the story because it not only reveals the character's awareness, it reveals something about him. The natural question from the reader is, 'Why is he noticing that?' and if it's only to give the reader information, [as this example is doing] it's in the wrong voice. It should be in the distant voice. When this happens, it jerks the reader out of that fictional reality you are creating and so destroys what you're trying to do. That is a major flaw. Here's an example from a short story, 'The Deterrent', of the third close voice in which the character is actively noticing the setting, giving it his personal stamp and stressing its importance, which is indicated by the line, "He found himself checking…"

A police van pulled to a stop in the single parking place next to the ticket booth. Jay looked from the van to the scaffold. He found himself checking the actual scene against the government pamphlet he had studied. As prescribed, the distance was one hundred yards. Ten yards away a hard packed dirt path from the van to the scaffold had been marked out with knee high wooden stakes painted white, and finger-thick cotton rope, broad enough for three men to walk abreast

Suddenly he heard something. A voice. From inside the van. And metallic pounding.

"NO! NO! NO! NO! NO!" The voice was mechanical, the hysteria at level pitch, as if the condemned man had succeeded in holding the horror to come at bay with his protest.

One more point here: any setting the author describes has some significance because the author decided to describe it or use it. But it's the emphasis through voice makes all the difference, i.e., great and varied detail using all five senses in the close or distant voice, implies a very important scene, however the same scene given a cursory description, and maybe just stressing the visual, becomes less important to the reader due to this lack of emphasis. It's could just be a reality scene. Of great significance in stressing or not stressing a setting, is the point of view, the voice. A scene from the third distant might be vivid and impressive, but the same scene from a close point of view has the advantage of being character based, and because character is story, that scene will become more significant.

What all this means is that you have to know when to use distant and when to use close voice in both points of view. Also be aware that shifting back and forth between the distant and close voices creates stylistic pace, which simply means the reader is given an impression of movement but there is no actual physical movement in the plot line. This is a critical technique to be aware of if you have a necessary, heavily informational bloc in your story because you can give the impression of action by, for example, shifting back and forth between the distant and close voices.

There is a very interesting and effective style of the third distant voice which is the third distant voice with an attitude. This is a voice that may or may not be the author's, but it is a distant voice, not a character, and it expresses attitudes about things in the story from the characters to the settings to situations, and sometimes reflects the character's reactions to these things.

In the following excerpt from my short story, 'The Shadow Witness," the distant voice is clear in the use of four similes, because figurative language is not something this character normally uses, but the similes do reflect his reactions to Lester, which is a distant voice with an attitude. The rest of the excerpt occupies that middle ground between close, "Lived with his mother. She took in ironing." and distant, "Lester used her…", with the distant voice dominant.

Memories of the child-man. Vague, emotional, surreal, intense. Rushing through the mind like an unexpected summer breeze, surprising, refreshing, ephemeral. And memories etched with anger, bitterness, and shame. Like a white hot nail in the heart.

Lester, rough punching fists, knuckles like canvas, the end of one finger blown off by a dynamite cap, wild, light brown hair always uncombed, tight smiles and eyes like nail heads, flicking, squinting, wary. Lived with his mother. She took in ironing. A retarded 35 year old sister who drooled and giggled. Wore loose cotton print dresses Walked barefoot down Cedar Ridge sidewalks, winter and summer. Lester used her to frighten his friends.

Use of figurative language is most often in the distant voice, but can be used in the close voice if that's a part of the character's personality. In either situation, the figurative language should be consistent with or accurately reflect the character. For example, in the preceding example, it would have been inconsistent to use urban or suburban images. They had to be more rural to be consistent with the character.

A final point about voice and character. In every scene in a story the idea of a focus character is critical. This is the character through whom the scene is seen or around whom the action takes place. Clearly the focus character is the most important in the scene, and most often it will be either the central character or a secondary character, but it can be any character. In third person voice novels, writers often use this focus character to give information to the reader that the central character doesn't have, but which the reader needs to know in order to understand what's going on. For example, in a crime novel, the author may shift the focus from the central character, to a secondary character, [say from the detective to the killer], in order to give the reader information the central character doesn't have, like motivation of the killer.

Here's an example of a shift in focus to a secondary character, Wiseman, around whom the action is focused, from my novel The Cold Warriors:

Wiseman continued to study him. "What union was it?"

"United Mine and Mill Workers, Local 541."

Wiseman frowned and looked away as if trying to recall something. Suddenly he looked back, his eyes wide with surprise. “Jesus! When you join a union you really go all out. Did you know they were on the Attorney General’s list?”

“Not when I joined it.”

“When did you find out?”

“When we went out on strike.” Matt looked at his hands, recalling the long, miserable months at the mine, the month he spent in jail.

Wiseman suddenly pushed himself up on both elbows and stared at Matt. “Wait a minute! Colorado, right? A couple of years ago, where was it, somewhere near Leadville?” He whistled. “Fuck me! I heard about it from my old man. He said it was just like the twenties all over again. The cops really beat the shit out of you guys.”

“Yeah, it was something, all right.”

“C’mon! Don’t play this Gary Cooper shit with me. Were you in the middle of all that?”

“Oh yeah, got the crap beat of me by scabs and company goons and the cops…”

Wiseman bounced up to a sitting position, a huge grin on his face. “Company goons! Scabs! Oh, fuck, my old man would love you!”

In the dialog, Wiseman dominates and his reactions to replies from the central character are given more emphasis, which indicate his reactions here are more important. He is the focus of the scene.

Here is an example of a character thorough whom the scene is seen, from my short story “The Dog Eaters:”

Simon watched him, fascinated. With his thumb and index finger, the Dog Eater continued to pluck the sardines out one by one, bringing them up in front of his eyes and then tilting his head back, he dropped the sardines in his mouth. The oil dribbled on his cheeks, and ran down his chin, sliding through his whiskers. He chewed a moment, slipped two more Ritz crackers in his mouth and munched away, looking out across the creek, ignoring Simon, looking at the high canyon wall opposite him, the can of sardines in one hand, the end of the torn paper tube of Ritz crackers sticking out of his coat pocket. The Dog Eater looked like he'd forgotten he was eating and was trying to recall something important.

Simon is a young boy who sees this but doesn't' really understand it. It's more important for the reader to know what Simon sees rather than what he understands about it, so the scene is focused through him, objectively, with no value judgments. My intention was to make the image as vivid as possible to imply what Simon remembers about the Dog Eater, so that later, when the Dog Eater is mentioned the reader knows what Simon recalls.

Basically, the focus character is the one in a scene given the most emphasis. This sounds easy and obvious, but many writers forget the idea of a focus character and, using a multiple close voice, give several characters in a single scene, equal emphasis, which makes the scene ambivalent or gives it a feeling of being unnecessary. This doesn't mean every scene requires a focus character, but if you're in a close voice, there does need to be a focus character. Distant voice is the voice of a scene without a focus character.

By this time your character should be taking on at least three dimensions for you. You know who they are, where they're from, some of why they are the way they are, etc. Now, putting them into action will begin to create that fourth dimension that they need. Here are some **exercises for the third person point of view:**

Using the third distant voice, introduce your central character to the reader in a setting in which the character is normally found. Be certain to create a concrete, physical image of the character in your reader's mind. If there are other people in the setting, make them background only. Remember in the distant voice you're not using the character's eye or reactions. It is the distant narrative voice giving as accurate a picture as possible of the place this character is normally found. For example, from my short story, "Rose:"

Rose, at ten, arms and legs like willow sticks, an abnormally round head, tiny eyes deep in her skull like black raisins poked too far into her face, stuck too close to her nose, a pale red skull covered with cobwebby hair the color of toast. It looked brittle almost as if one touched it, it would break off like dry twigs.

She never spoke. At first, teachers tried to pull words out of her, but she remained mute.

"Rose dear," Mrs. Beesome would say, "would you please read the paragraph on page five, aloud?"

She would lower her head, fix her eyes on the desk top, and her neck flushed red.

She smelled musty and thick, like an old damp closet left shut too long. She lived in a shack near Surface Creek with her parents and two brothers, and twenty yards behind the shack was an outhouse. People said they had seen her, early in the morning, bathing in the creek. The soap foam drifted downstream. She heard people on the bridge laugh, but it not as if it were funny.

Write the scene as it comes to you through your understanding of the character, the way you see it develop in your mind's eye. Then, once you've got the raw material down, go back and begin to shape it.

A word here about "overwriting." You're probably going to overwrite just about anything you attempt, but that's good. This means in your rewrite, you're editing back, which always tightens the story and makes it better. Adding scenes, etcetera usually bogs the story line down and destroys the pace. What this means is when you're on first or second draft of a story, just let it flow, don't worry about length. Get as much out as you can and then edit. Detailed editing as you go is a good way to destroy a story.

If it helps in writing a scene, imagine yourself as a camera with five senses, plus intelligence and sensitivity. Think of close ups, long shots, panoramic views. Think of the organization of your scene, left to right, top to bottom, most important to least important, and vice versa, and how you want your reader to see this scene and why that way. All of this is to accomplish one thing; to introduce your character to a reader.

Once you've written your introduction of the character, take the same scene and put it in close third person, the character's voice, and reveal the scene through your character's way of seeing the world, their choice of details, their vocabulary, etc. What the distant voice revealed may not be what the character notices or how s/he notices it. This is the difference between your fictional reality as it exists [distant voice] and the way your character sees that reality, [close voice].

SETTING

Setting is, above all else, a sense of place that demands specific sensory details, but it is quite a bit more than that. Specific names of things, objects, places, flora, fauna, all make your fictional world vivid and give it an intense reality. Without these specific details, your setting is simply generic, i.e., it could be anywhere, at anytime, it has no depth. For example, here is a scene submitted to one of my fiction workshops:

The log cabin faced west and was located next to the creek. A tree next to the cabin had fallen that winter and it stretched from the side of the cabin down to the water's edge. There were bushes growing wild on both sides of the cabin, and a thick grove of trees served as a windbreak behind the cabin. From the front step, on a clear day, you could see the mountain range fifty miles away. It was very isolated.

So what's the problem?? First of all, where is this place, other than in a rural setting? There are no clues, no specific names of vegetation, of the landmarks such as the river or the mountain range. How far from the river is the cabin? A tree's length? Okay, what kind of tree? Is it a palm tree? A dwarf pine? An oak? The reader has no idea of how large the tree is or even what kind it is, so there are no clues there. "It was very isolated" is telling something but it's much too vague. Now here's the rewrite:

The roughly hewn log cabin sat on the northwest slope of the Kuskokwim Range, looking toward the Kaiyuh Mountains about seventy five miles away. Some forty miles to the northwest was the town of Poorman, where she usually went for supplies every two or three months, and once a year she went south to Iditarod, just to watch the annual dog sled race .

The top twenty feet of a hundred foot Douglas fir on the north side of the cabin had snapped off during a blizzard that winter, and fallen toward Raven Creek fifty yards in front of the cabin. She had trimmed the branches of the fall earlier that spring, sawed the thick trunk into two foot sections, then split them into quarters and stacked them under the cabin eaves, filling the cabin with the sharp, clean smell of pine sap. Behind the cabin, the thick windbreak of white birch had, as always, weathered the winter nicely and was now leafed out in a soft spring green. A light breeze rustled through the birch leaves bringing a whisper of summer warmth. The Gambel oak on both sides of the cabin was just beginning to show some green and soon would be an almost impenetrable thicket when the sharp leaves had fully bloomed.

The scene now is much more specific in terms of place, and with the identification of trees and bushes, as well as specific names of rivers, towns and mountain ranges, the scene becomes this scene, and no other. Also the place names have a flavor to them and lend an aura of wilderness to the scene. You don't want to overload a scene with sensory details, but there are no sensory details in the original, which means the writer is appealing only to the intellect. Adding colors, shapes, sizes, smells and sound to the description, bring it to life.

Here's an example of overdoing a scene with details:

The sweet smell of Chanel # 5 wafted out of the vintage Rolls Royce Silver Cloud as the woman, dressed in a gold Versace gown, seated on the rolled leather upholstery the color of Cancun sand, looked out the open window of the back seat as she removed one flawless pearl earring, and pressed the Nokia cell phone to her shell like ear.

It sounds like an uber yuppie catalog, to say nothing of the cliché ear at the end. For a writer who has an incredible sense of place, read Ivan Doig's English Creek or House of Sky or Ride With Me Mariah Montana. In his novels, the setting is so strongly developed it becomes a character itself.

A writer has to have a sensitivity to the place of his/her fictional world and be able to convey not only the physical-sensory details of the place, but a sense of what it is like emotionally, from depressing or desperate to idyllic. Without that added fourth dimension, the setting will just be a pale imitation of reality. Most often, when you're trying to convey the emotional impact of a setting, you would go with the close, [character's] voice, but the author's reaction to the setting is also very important and that comes through in the way the distant voice describes a setting.

Here's an example of a setting given through the third person close voice, from a short story of mine "The Great American Car:"

The plan: drive The Great American Car, [a 1967 Dodge Dart Slant 6], [should have been a horse] to the Texas Bar where his good acquaintance, [got no friends] Fletcher hangs out. Place sounds hollow when you walk in. Smells like a Pine-Sol factory test site. Makes him wonder what new germ or old smell they're trying to kill or cover up. The only modern thing in the place is the Rock-Ola juke box. Squatting in one corner. All chrome and plastic and hard angles. Like a UFO in a cathedral. Playing Lefty Frizzell for Christ's sake. A real time warp.

The idea in the first part of the scene is to give the reader an impression of the setting, but more importantly, to reveal something about the narrator's values and personality. In the second part, there is more real detail, as opposed to emotionally charged detail, and the shift in syntax implies that as well:

A long bar with no bar stools on the left side of the door was lined with regular drinkers, all standing, hunched over their bottles of Bud and shot glasses of Jose Cuervo, standing because the Texas Bar doesn't fuck around about drinking. Purity of purpose. Sometimes called drink till you drop. A few high backed wooden booths on the opposite wall. Painted shit brown. Like the walls. No women in the place, not in the light of day. Thank god. The juke box thumps away, playing more Lefty, punctuated by the click and thump of two snooker players in the back.

Let me reiterate: use specific names for things like trees or flowers or animals, but don't overdo it. What you want to do is find the most effective specific name that gives not only clear information, but has an emotional impact as well. That doesn't mean an extreme emotional reaction, but it should create something more than a simple intellectual understanding of the scene. To achieve this, you select the details you want to emphasize and leave the others clear but non emphatic. For instance, in the previous example, I used Lefty Frizzell to give it emphasis, but I could have left it general by simply using 'a country western singer.' By using Lefty Frizzell, the implications are more complex, i.e., he was a singer popular in the 1950s, known for hard core country ballads, and his main rival was Hank Williams. Some readers will know all that, and the name serves as a trigger for a multitude of reactions. Other readers, probably most of them, only realize the name is specific but have no real knowledge of what the name means, but if they're curious, another level of meaning opens up for them.

The central idea of creating a setting with such care, is to develop such a powerful sense of place that your reader loses him/herself in your fictional world. This is more than just using the five senses, although that is the basic element in creating a fictional reality. Setting also involves a feeling for the setting, either from the distant voice or from the character or both. Absolutely critical in any description is the logical flow of the details. If the details jump back and forth or without any clear logic, the impact is destroyed.

Use of Real World Settings: Even if you're using an actual place as your setting, it's still your fictional world because you're making the choices of what and how to describe it, which means you're enhancing the setting, not simply describing reality. It's important to remember you're not writing a travelogue. You can do what you want with the real setting, from moving a place from one part of the country to another, or simply imposing your fictional world on a real place, as Faulkner did with Yoknapatawpha County.

For example, here's the opening scene from my novel Ashes To The Wind:

He could see old man Yanovich's dog trotting down Main Street past the courthouse, Brown's grocery, Eckhard's Department Store, then across the street to snuffle at a pickup's tire in front of the feed store, finally trotting around the corner into the alley where Morris and he had turpentined a cat twelve years ago. Nothing else moved in Cedar Ridge.

This is an actual town in Colorado recreated from my memory of it as a nine or ten year old child, but enhanced in order to recreate it as the town in my novel. One of the strongest reactions I got about that novel, was that the place was so real that it permeated the story line as well, giving it the aura of truth, which is what I wanted. That is one major point about creating strong settings; it lends an aura of truth to the events. In writing fiction, one goal is to convince the reader that this could have happened, not that it did happen, and setting helps you do that.

It's fairly apparent that characterization and point of view directly effect setting and vice versa. If you're in first person, the setting becomes absolutely critical in revealing the character as h/she relates it to the reader. Remember, in first person the only source of information for the reader, is your character/narrator. For example, from my short story, "The Fire Runner" here is a passage in first person, describing a scene:

I am an Old Man, one who gravitates toward the peaks. Scrabbles amongst granite boulders capped with golden lichen, and higher, on the barren, wind-blasted summits above timberline. I find the windless pockets. Scoop out small pits and build fires of twigs and curl my body around the warmth. Tendrils of pungent pine smoke soak into my clothing, my skin. My eyes roam over the far blue-black ridge lines below me. The miraculous, gravity-defying stands of fir trees grip the steep slopes like thick, dark hair. Down near the river, in the depths of the sun starved canyons, cold sound echoes senselessly. Pock marked snow lies in shadowed ravines like crumbling scabs.

I turn my face to the four points and see the few places I have been and the many I have not. One after the other, the ridges slant in from the north and south, like a series of knife blades, looking as if a man could leap from one to the other, until they end on the dim horizon with nothing behind the final peak but pale blue sky. Here, above timberline, the air is thin and pure. At night the sky is white with stars, galaxies. The red edge of the universe trembles and fills me with fear. My soul aches with clarity.

I wanted this scene to be vivid to the reader, but even more I wanted the Old Man to reveal the kind of person he was by how he described the setting.

In third person close voice, your character is where s/he is because of something in them and they are there by choice or not, which will affect the way they see the setting in opposition to the way the distant voice relates it to the reader. Always keep in mind that the distant voice is the voice of fictional reality, but the close voice is the voice of personal truth, how the character perceives the fictional reality. Here is a setting done in third person distant, from my short story, "The Corn Field:"

Walking past an unpainted wood slab door set in an ancient, crumbling basalt wall overgrown with wild golden marigolds; the gnarled limbs of old fruit trees in fragrant white and pink blossom lean across the top of the wall, overhanging the narrow rutted lane, the crumbling wall descending from head to shoulder to waist, revealing tables of white wood, straight backed wooden chairs painted red and blue and green, a roadside cafe under an open-sided, palm-thatched roof; early Sunday afternoon, several couples sit, sipping glasses of maize beer, murmuring contentedly under the drone of insects, the raucous call of unseen birds, and soft laughter. The familiar sound of gunfire is, for the moment, gone.

And here is an example of the third person, close voice, describing a setting from my short story, "The Land of Make Believe:"

He visits the Quail Ridge Shopping Center, aware of where he is sitting; in a orange plastic pseudo sidewalk cafe, in a temperature controlled mall, an eternal seventy-six degrees Fahrenheit, hearing the muzak hum soothingly just below the level of consciousness, eyes unstrained by the scientifically controlled indirect lighting, mind eased by psychologically compatible pastel color schemes of peach and lemon and papaya, drinking automatically made instant coffee out of an orange plastic cup, watching people move along scientifically determined traffic flow patterns, searching for a flash of humanity somewhere, oozing out from under all these layers of products, and finally, finally, some-anonymous-one silently farts leaving a thick, almost tangible cloud of intestinal gas drifting behind. He smiles. A catalyst. People's eyes shifting nervously back and forth, hands flying up to cover noses, mouths, someone coughs, another snickers, a score of tiny human gestures and sounds bursting forth, then as quickly, disappear. He toys with the idea of tracking down the phantom farter, sniffing after him/her until he reaches the source of this gaseous, intestinal Nile that leaves small waves of humanity eddying out behind in this teeming cavern of lifelessness.

If you want the reader to react strongly to the setting, and you're in third person, you have to decide how much is going to come through your character [close voice] and how much through the narrator [distant voice]. The character's attitude toward the place they find themselves in, has a lot to do with what voice you're going to use to describe it. For example, if the character hates the setting, but you want the reader to have a truthful look at it, then you go to the distant voice. If it's more important that the reader understand the character's attitude about the setting, then you go to close voice.

If you just want the reader to have clear informational details on the setting, you stay in distant voice. As the writer, you have to decide if you want an objective [distant] or subjective [close] view of the setting, and where you want one or the other. Changing the voice describing the setting causes a major shift in impact for the reader.

You can shift between the distant and close voice, going from emotional [close] to intellectual [distant], depending upon what reaction you want to create in your reader, remembering there also has to be a logical flow to the voices, i.e., why the close voice suddenly, then a shift back to the distant, etcetera.

Try this: Create an action scene in which the third distant voice describes the setting of the action, then shift to the third close voice, the character involved in the action, and describe what's happening in that voice. Make it around 500 words, about two pages double spaced, and let the distant voice dominate. Here's an example of that shift from third distant to third close from my novel, The Touchmaster's Network:

The scaffold kit gleamed like a obsidian cube, gathering pre-dawn dew on the grass of Greenplace 43. A curious squirrel scampered up, sniffed the black plastic components and with a flick of its tail, dashed off and disappeared into the tall willows of the creek. Across the valley the sun eased up over Mount Quayle, the first rays illuminating the white lettering on the black plastic: PROPERTY OF THE CRIMINAL VIGILANCE COMMITTEE.

Park use began at 0600, however at this hour, the only human activity inside Greenplace 43 were the Park Patrols. Weekday use was restricted to those citizens who lived within the city limits of Los Gatos, the weekends from 0800 to sunset being set aside for the lesser class designations who lived outside the city limits. At 0600 only Class I and II citizens were allowed in Greenplace 43.

Jay C. Phipps pulled his Geolectric, up to the guard station at the entrance to Greenplace 43, leaned out the window and pressed his left palm up against the I.D. plate. A second passed, the gate swung open and he drove through into the parking lot. Several people were doing stretching exercises next to their vehicles. He glanced around at the other Geolectrics parked there, looking for some familiar faces but saw no one he knew. He walked across the parking lot to a green uniformed Park Patrol guard who stood next to a second I.D. plate mounted on a steel post. Jay pressed his left palm against it and waited as the guard watched the small TV screen on his side of the post. A moment passed, and the guard nodded him through.

Jay was thankful that as a politically correct teacher he rated a Class II designation and was allowed to use the park between six and seven thirty in the morning. He hated running in the heat and even worse were the crowds of Class III (married professionals with one child), Class IV (semi professional families with two children) and Class V (men and women over 60) who crowded the paths all day and made running nearly impossible. At least at six in the morning the only obstacles were the Class I idiots who were allowed to have a dog. You had to be alert to dodge them when they were scooping poop into the little red bags the Park Patrol provided at the entrance the park. The limits on waste production were very strict and he often wondered how much the dog owners had to give up in terms of producing garbage in order to own a dog. Putting your name on a bag of dog shit and having it registered with a Park Patrol guard before you left was one bit of humiliation he could do without. Still, everyone knew if you had a dog, you were Class I and that was one of the few status symbols left for the privileged.

There may also be secondary, minor and back ground characters in the scene. By going back and forth between the two voices, you'll create a scene that is clear and that is also emotionally charged. By letting the distant voice dominate, you're stressing clarity. If you let the close voice dominate, you're stressing the emotional impact. The choice depends upon how you want the reader to react, i.e., intellectually by understanding what's going on, or emotionally, by going through the event with the character. The important thing to remember here is that if you're in close voice, the action, if you want it to be realistic, is going to be chaotic and emotional. You can't have a character involved in a fight, for example, and be acutely aware of his surroundings. Well, maybe you can, but then you've got some kind of psychotic on your hands. Here's an example of an action scene from a third distant point of view, from my short story, "The Shadow Witness:"

Lester slowly swaggered to the center of the lawn. The crowd slipped rapidly around to the left and right, leaving a ten yard no-man's-land between them and the two figures they encircled, ready to close the circle once the Indian kid moved toward Lester.

And he moved. Shoulders heaving once as if trying to breath, walking toward Lester. Who waited, boxer-poised, left shoulder dipped forward, left fist held out at eye level, left foot flat on the grass, sliding forward, right foot back, balanced on the toe, knees bent slightly, bouncing, right fist cocked close to his right shoulder, elbows tucked in, protecting his stomach. A classic fighting pose.

Lester leaped at him, hit him in the face. The Indian kid fell back, stunned, unprepared. Lester crowded closer, hit him in the stomach, in the face, left hand alternating with right, the Indian kid's head slewed around, his face grotesquely mashed, his body flung out of control, and the crowd screamed, "Get him Lester, kill him Lester!"

Write the same action scene you've just done, but now let the close voice dominate. And finally, write the same scene once more, shifting back and forth between the two voices.

The scenes done in the close and distant voices will reveal to you just what the most essential details of the scene are because the dominating voice [close] won't be able to clearly see them, so when the distant voice steps in, interrupting the action, it has to be with details that enhance the scene rather than interrupt it.

In an action scene, if you're in distant voice, the stress is on the general scene, from the setting to other characters, not the action, thus the action becomes a secondary enhancement of the scene. If the distant voice goes on too long it will destroy the action, the drama of the story.

FIRST PERSON POINT OF VIEW AND SETTING

The difficulty of this double first person voice [close and distant] is understanding just who the speaker is or should be. Keep it simple; the first person distant voice is the voice of the character recollecting the story, thus h/she knows what happened and is recreating the events, the place, the other people involved, from memory. This voice is deliberate and conscious of relating the story to the reader and consciously creates it for the reader. The distant voice wants to be understood clearly. However, because you're in first person, the recollection is going to be flawed, it's going to be skewed to fit the narrator's version of the events, which may be real, but not necessarily truthful. As in all first person stories, it is a story of character, so how this first person distant voice recollects the events of the story, also reveals that character's personality. You have to decide on just how reliable or unreliable you want this character to be.

The first person close voice is the voice of the character at the time of the story, the same person who is telling you this, but instead of looking back on the events, this voice is involved in the events as they occur. The close voice character is unaware of how these events turn out, and is simply going through the events as they happen. It is the voice of action, surprise, shock. If there is a major difference in age between the distant and the close voice, then there's also going to be a difference in syntax and vocabulary, and that would be one way to differentiate between the two voices.

I need to repeat something here because it's an important aspect of gaining control of your writing. You are going to be shifting back and forth between the two voices, and how much time you spend in each voice will be determined by the impact you want the story to have on your reader. Simply put, if you want an intellectual appreciation, you let the distant voice dominate. If you want an emotional response, you go with the close voice. This is another case of gaining control, i.e., if you know how you want your reader to react, you'll know which voice to emphasize. It's not a hit and miss affair, or at least it shouldn't be.

This means that structure is going to be one of the critical considerations in setting up a first person story. For example, if you wanted the reader's reaction to be dominantly emotional, a logical structure would be to use the close voice for most of the story, using the distant voice to frame it, say at the opening, setting the scene, and then shifting to the close voice and then at the conclusion, going back to the distant voice to end it.

SHOWING VS. TELLING

I'm sure you've all heard this "rule" in one form or another, but the most common cliché is, "Show, don't tell," which means action is the basis for fiction, not exposition. Basically it's true because stories that engage readers, appeal to the emotions, the senses, and have characters acting and interacting. What happens with showing dominating, is the creation of a fictional reality that readers can lose themselves in, but there is a place for telling in every story and the emphasis depends upon the effect you want to create for and/or in your reader.

Before we get into details about showing versus telling, it must be emphasized that any discussion of this topic naturally includes voice, that is distant and close voice. It's impossible to separate voice and showing and telling, therefore I'm going to make frequent references to voice as it is used in showing or telling. Two things should result from this focus: you become much more familiar with the idea of voice, and you understand how to use showing and/or telling as a more complex technique than it appears on the surface.

Simply stated, close voice is showing and distant voice is telling. For example:

Telling: *James walked downtown through the August heat. He was* *hot and uncomfortable.*

Here the proper name James sets up the distant voice, and thereafter, it is strictly informational with no detailed sensory input.

Showing: *James walked downtown. August in Arizona. He could feel the heat from the sidewalk burning up through the soles of his Reboks, and his thin cotton shirt, damp with sweat, stuck to his chest. He plucked at it with his thumb and index finger, lifting it away from his chest for that momentary flash of coolness.*

In the previous example, the personal pronoun 'he' immediately after the opening line which identifies James, sets up the close voice and after that the details become more specifically sensory and personal.

If you want a dominantly intellectual reaction, then you would go for a voice that explains, examines, considers and analyzes. Telling, is talking about what's happening, telling or explaining to the reader something, not showing them. For example, here's a distant third person voice telling of events from the central character's youth in a short story of mine entitled "Pasadena:"

Livingston didn't understand the six months he'd spent in Pasadena, living alone in an old Victorian rooming house, just three blocks up from Colorado Boulevard. He had no idea why he had been there, or even how he somehow or other got a job as a shipping clerk for Sol, a Tupperware distributor, a man who, every year, won a new Cadillac for selling enough Tupperware to justify his own shipping point. Livingston wondered what had he been doing there, and why he cared now, as he closed rapidly in on the final decades of his actuarial life?

In the previous paragraph, the opening lines are telling in third person distant voice, set up through the character's name, "Livingston" and after that the voice remains distant, telling of his reactions and giving information to the reader about this experience, the where and who of this situation. The tone is explanatory and informational, thus telling.

In the following paragraph there is a shift to showing the character's thoughts and reactions through the close voice, such as using rhetorical questions which is a more personal reaction. Further examples of the showing voice is the more personal style in vocabulary and syntax, as in the use of the vernacular, and the details here also become much more specific, creating a concrete image rather than an intellectual understanding of the situation. In this showing paragraph, the proper name "Livingston" disappears and the personal pronoun "he" replaces it, another indication of the close voice.

It was easy to recall the images he had, even now, of hundreds of hopeful housewives pounding the pavement, holding Tupperware parties every night so this guy, this snappy dresser with a handkerchief in his jacket pocket that matched his socks, but not, thank god, the wide, garish ties of orange and green and yellow flowers, could drive a new Caddy every year. He could recall how Sol's two tone brown and white shoes clicked when he walked from the heel taps. Why heel taps? And Sol had, for god's sake, a pencil thin moustache, he was a living cliché. He could forgive all that sartorial splendor if only Sol hadn't worn his cream colored suit coat draped over his shoulders, like some Latin lover out of a Turner Classic 1940s movie. That, and the cigars he smoked, giant cigars that jutted obscenely out of his mouth, like a penis on fire, yes, that's what it had to be, a goddamn smoking brown prick.

His use of the simile, 'like a Latin lover out of a Turner Classic 1940s movie,' comes from him, as do the exclamations such as 'for God's sake.' In the final line the showing voice describes the cigars, going from slightly proper, "a penis," to totally vernacular, a "prick," with both of them being highly personal reactions, thus, showing.

The two paragraphs work together, moving from telling in the first, which establishes the situation and scene which I want the reader to understand, and then showing in the second, to move the reader into the scene with the character because I want an emotional reaction to what the character is recalling.

A combination of the telling and showing voices is fairly common in most fiction, and most writers probably do it from instinct for what the story needs to make it live for the reader. In order to gain control of that "instinct" you have to be aware of the two voices and what makes them different. Basically the close voice emotes, the distant voice reports.

Remember, a non emotional voice describing a scene accurately can create an emotion in the reader by vivid description of details, which is the difference in creating an emotion in the reader, and creating an emotion in your character.

Here is an example of creating an emotion in the reader through telling, from my short story, "The Last Image In A Dead Man's Eyes:"

J.D.'s daily walk from Esteban's house, a scant twenty-five yards off the plaza, was slow and measured, much slower than mere physical limitations would dictate. J.D. would stop frequently, looking out across the tin roofs of the low adobe houses built on a narrow ridge that fell steeply away toward the river valley far below, toward the small patchwork fields outside the village, each field a subtly different shade of green, and beyond them, to the dark dusty green of pinons on sandy brown earth. He seemed to savor the landscape, as one rolled fine wine over the tongue.

Or his nostrils would flare when a young woman came walking barefooted up the street as if he were catching the essence of her life as she passed by.

J.D. ran his fingers over the rough-hewn wooden benches worn smooth by use and time, or along the hand-made adobe bricks of the village houses, as if feeling their solidity, the night coolness on his palm as the morning sun warmed the back of his hand.

Sometimes J.D. would hunch his shoulders so that his bones cracked and then he would stretch his neck, twisting his head slowly like an animal savoring the sun's heat. He even brushed the huge, fat, droning, horse flies away from his face as if they were partially welcome.

In the previous example, the repeated use of the character's name, J.D., keeps the scene objective and distant, the telling voice, and although the sensory details are vivid, they are not coming through the character, but from a distant voice that is telling of the scene. The narration is totally external, that is, outside the character, and at three points a simile is used to stress the telling nature of the scene, i.e., "as if catching," "as if feeling" and "like an animal." If there were no similes there, it would be in the character's mind, thus showing.

In the next example the distant voice tells the reader what the character is seeing through his camera as he photographs the scene. The idea in this paragraph is to put the reader in the same state of mind as the character, in both cases, striving for distance from the horror. From The Touchmaster's Network:

Jay pointed the lens to the rear of the truck and adjusted the focus. Something was falling out. Jay jerked his head away from the camera in shock, then quickly sighted back in. Bodies came tumbling out of the rear of the truck. Some naked, some half clothed, all of them oddly stiff, flopping, arms waving suddenly as they tumbled out of the truck and down the slope into the dirt trench. Jay shot, advanced the film, shot, advanced the film, refocused, shot, advanced the film, heads flopped loosely as the bodies tumbled from the back of the truck, shoot, advance the film, a tangle of arms, legs, heads spilled out over the metal lip of the truck, shoot, refocus, advance, shoot, they fell loosely, limply, eyes, mouths, faces all alike in death, empty, ageless now, already skeletal. Arms, legs, torsos, heads tangled, piled, a chaos of death.

The hydraulic ram clanged loudly against the lip of the truck, the engine slowed, idled. The outrider walked to the back of the truck, peered in, then stepped back and waved at the driver who was watching him in the rear view mirror.

"Okay. Everything's out." He grabbed the handle at the rear of the truck and swung up on the riding platform as the truck roared away from the dump site.

The character's reaction was a desperate need to not react to the horror he was seeing, and the device the character used to do that was the camera. In this scene, the details were deliberately non descriptive, more telling than showing, totally visual, which also stresses the camera. No other sensory input was used, other than the "hydraulic ram clanged" to end the scene. Thus, you have a non emotional voice telling of a horrific scene, to create the same emotional reaction in both character and reader.

In the following example of showing, the first person close voice tells the reader about this scene, again consciously trying to maintain distance and control. From my novel, God's Waltz:

The entry hall was cool, with twelve inch square, red dairy tiles on the floor, but something had been spilled or splashed on them, leaving darker stains everywhere. I looked at the walls. More of the same. It looked as if Jackson Pollock on a wild drunk had taken a huge paint brush, dipped it in whatever this was, and then spun around, letting it fly out in great splatters. Framed oils and water colors had been knocked askew and various ob'jets d'art, from silver candlesticks to Indian baskets were strewn everywhere.

I glanced at Chris. His face was pale. He looked back at me and silently shook his head. On the floor were large swatches as if someone had swept a mop soaked with a dark liquid, over the tiles. And footprints, someone wearing waffle soled hiking boots. I was pretty sure what I was looking at when I smelled something unfamiliar and familiar. Thick, coppery, bitter. Chris looked at me, his lips parted slightly, breathing though his mouth to avoid the smell. I did the same.

Showing is dominantly action. If you have information you want the reader to have, but you don't want it drawn out in a long narrative, dialog is the dramatic way to get the information across because dialog is pure showing.

In the following excerpt the dialog was used to show rather than tell, how teachers were reacting to being required to take their students to a public execution, from my novel, The Touchmaster's Network:

"I've never seen a man killed before." Bud said suddenly.

Jay glanced at him. "Me either. And the idea still doesn't do anything for me."

"God help me, I think I want to see it."

"What?" Jay's voice was quiet, as if he didn't want to understand what he knew he had heard. "I hope you aren't bringing a video camera. That's going too far for a lesson plan, Bud."

He shook his head. "No, nothing like that, but, there's something, fascinating about it. Now, I mean. You know, it's not a reality yet. It's just a fantasy, like your own death seems to be."

"It won't be fantasy in a couple of hours." Jay stopped at the classroom next to Bud's.

"'Ask not for whom the bell tolls.'" Bud smiled weakly.

Jay nodded. He knew someone was going to quote Donne today and he had made damned sure it wasn't him. He pressed his palm against the i.d. plate, the door whooshed open and he walked into the classroom. The class filed in quickly, logged in on their CRTs, then looked expectantly at him. Jay nodded. "Lesson plan for today: Crime and Punishment. Okay folks, let's go."

Showing involves the reader on a more visceral level, and you go with either a first person close or third person close, voice. This close voice doesn't automatically mean that you are stressing action if all the character does is think or talk about acting. For example, a character telling about climbing K-2:

"We made the final assault about two in the afternoon and after several hours of struggling in the snow and ice, we were exhausted and turned back."

And how exciting and involving was that? You understand what happened, but you don't see it, feel it or experience it in any way. If this event was unimportant, then it's right to tell of it in that manner. If, however it was important, then you've got to show it.

One basic rule of thumb with showing and telling; if there is something the reader absolutely needs to understand, and which can't conveniently be shown, tell them. For example: The scars on his face were a result of a childhood sledding accident.

Another use of telling rather than showing is when there is information the characters are exchanging but which the reader is already aware of, you summarize by telling. For example, if your character has had an unusual experience which the reader has already seen, but a character in the story is not aware of, you summarize it: 'He told her about the nasty stewardess on his flight home.'

Fiction demands more showing than telling, but telling is a very useful device in many instances. The thing that's tricky about showing vs. telling is that many beginning writers unconsciously accept the idea of 'Tell me a story,' and immediately launch off into a totally telling mode, which is boring at best. If you keep in mind the two voices [distant and close] of the two points of view [first and third], you won't fall into the telling trap. A simple rule of thumb is this: close voice is 99% showing any time it's used because the information is coming through the character and so is biased. Any time the character 'tells' the reader something, he or she is revealing something about themselves, thus, showing.

Distant voice is more a 'pure' telling voice because it does have objectivity. The difference between showing and telling in the distant voice is the intensity of sensory detail used. Basically, the clearer the image becomes is an indication of a showing distant voice. This brings up a major point of confusion in showing vs telling. The idea of a distant voice describing a scene, looks and sounds like telling, not action, but if it's done carefully, it is still showing. For example, from my novel, The Ghost Dancers II:

It was the silence of the city that emptied souls of hope for the final time. The realization that there would never, could never be a return to things the way they had been finally hit home. No one could have been ready for that, could have been prepared for the gray, motionless silence that seemed to have frozen San Francisco, like all American cities, into moonscape immobility.

And then from this emotional, psychological set-up the distant voice moves to more physical, general details:

And with the silence, a part of it, was the almost total lack of movement, the flowing energy of a city alive that one feels as much as sees. Nothing human moved. Seagulls swooped and glided, rats scrabbled, dog packs trotted down the middle of once car crowded streets.

Now the voice is focusing in on more specific details:

*Before, driving into The City, the skyscraper skylines were alive, generating vibrations of activity. Time and temperature signs blinked and slowly revolved Stock market averages flashed on top of bank buildings. The red-yellow-green-white neon signs that announced EAT, SAFEWAY, MACY*S, GUMP'S were dead. No street lights clicked, no office lights burned, there were no horns honking, radios blaring, no whirring clicking sound of the cables under the streets pulling the cable cars up the steep hill on Powell, no ships sailing on the bay. The twisting curving sweeps of freeway exchanges were empty, like veins suddenly drained of life's blood. The city was a corpse.*

Or, more accurately, almost a corpse. The death throes were not quite finished. Occasional gun shots echoed up and down the desolate, weed grown streets. A scream that could be animal or human. Glass shattering. A dark, furtive figure dashing across an empty, littered street and into a building. Something or someone scuttling around a corner.

An alternative to this in a "pure," telling voice would read like this:

The city was silent. There were no sounds or movement that indicated human life. No lights. There were no ships on the bay. The streets and freeways were empty. There were, however, sounds of death and dying, a gun shot, a scream, glass shattering, a dark figure running across an empty street and into a building.

Both are telling, with the first one using more sensory detail to make the scene 'live.' If, however, that scene had been given through a character, it would have been close voice and showing. For example:

Jay shook his head. It was the black and white silence of the city that emptied his soul of hope for the final time. The gaudy reds, yellows and greens of neon signs were gone. Billboards were tattered, turned gray with rain. The colors that did remain, metal signs, gas pumps, store fronts, were faded and stained. He knew no one could have been ready for that, could have been prepared for the gray, motionless silence that seemed to have frozen San Francisco, like all American cities, into moonscape immobility.

To continue with the close voice is simply a matter of continuing to use more of the vernacular and continue with the personal pronouns and the character's name. In this case, I made the decision that I wanted a distant voice to enhance the cold, dead atmosphere of the setting. I used some close voice techniques however, by using colors, specific place names, and as the view closes in, specific details, but I deliberately did not use smell which is a very close voice sensory detail.

The structure was also a part of this, going from general in the first paragraph to very specific in the next to last paragraph, and then back to general again in the final paragraph. It's obvious that a pure telling or pure showing voice, is infrequently used. Mostly it's a combination, with one of them dominating, depending upon the effect you want the setting to have on the reader.

Showing, however, is the basic technique for establishing a strong sense of place. Without the sensory details, and the human reaction to a place, it is simply an intellectual reality. Showing adds the dimension of emotion, of humanity. Another way of putting it is this: knowing = telling; experiencing = showing.

The usual point of view for strong setting is third or first distant for a very logical reason; if the central character is involved in something that takes all his/her attention, then it would be unbelievable that they would notice the details of the setting in which the action takes place. For example, I have two characters lost in a blizzard, who stumble across a shelter. The distant voice describes what they see, but it wouldn't be believable that in their numbed, half frozen condition, they would actively notice these details. What happens here is that the reader realizes this is what they are seeing, but not how they are seeing it. From my novel, The Ghostdancers II:

They led their horses and pack animals over to the cabin, which turned out to be three walls, about a dozen thick logs in height, leaning haphazardly inward. The fourth wall was a dirt embankment, and the roof was made of several criss-crossed layers of smaller logs over which sod had been placed. A crazily warped door frame was the only opening, the door long since gone. There were huge spaces between the logs, the mud chinking crumbled over the years allowing gusts of wind to whistle through the cracks. But it was shelter.

Inside the cabin consisted of one small room with a six foot ceiling and a floor of hard packed earth. A fifty gallon oil drum with a large opening cut into one side and a metal stove pipe fixed to the other sat against one wall. The stove pipe stuck out through another hole cut in the side of the cabin.

By the same token, if a character doesn't have the ability or nature to notice details of a setting, then the distant voice has to do that, which also means you're not in first person close. Or shouldn't be.

A sidelight to the close-distant p.o.v. is that you might have a first person distant voice, recreating a scene from memory, and if the scene comes across as positive, but the experience was negative, you have an interesting tension set up in the character. For example, from my short story collection, "The White Stag Rooms:" *[A word of explanation is necessary here; this is first person distant voice, and the 'Ted' referred to is the name of the narrator, who maintains a distant attitude toward himself and his experiences. In fact, he refers to himself as 'the narrator.' The story takes place in a psychiatric half way house called*

The White Stag Rooms]

Ted lives in the former music room on the first floor. It also had a sliding oak door with brass handles which was also removed between 1950 and 1970. Ted's room is a few feet down the narrow hall that runs from the front door to the rear of the house, into the kitchen.

It is simply furnished. Old prune boxes stacked and nailed floor to ceiling on three walls and filled with books and various objects. Each wall is divided into eras of history devised by Ted, starting with pre-history and running to 1945. The fourth wall is devoted to the era 1945 to NOW. Ted was born on July 16, 1945, the day the first A-bomb was exploded in Alamogordo, New Mexico. A true baby boomer. Almost all the boxes on the fourth wall contain objects.

A copper colored, down sleeping bag is placed precisely in the center of the room. One bare, one hundred watt light bulb hangs down over the sleeping bag. A large night watchman's flashlight and a Big Ben alarm clock sit next to the sleeping bag. The windows are blocked out by the prune box shelves, so the light is, at best, dim during the day and it is pitch black at night.

At night, Ted is awakened by the alarm clock every hour, all night long. He sits up in the sleeping bag, turns on the flashlight and methodically moves the beam all around the room looking at each wall of boxes from the floor to the ceiling. Once he has checked them all, he resets the alarm, flicks off the flashlight and goes back to sleep.

My idea here was to take a fictional technique, distant first person p.o.v., and make it part of this character's attempt to rebuild his sanity. In the story, he not only narrates his own life, he narrates the lives of those other inmates in The White Stag Rooms with him. This shows you what you can do with something as basic as voice.

For a little practice here,

Create an action scene in which the third person distant voice describes [shows, as in the Ghost Dancers II example] the setting of the action, then shift the focus to the third close voice, the character involved in the action. Create a structure in which distant voice frames the action, with the action as the dominant point. Make it around 300 words.

In a rewrite shift the emphasis by stressing the scene in the distant voice, with the action as enhancement.

Do the same thing with the first distant and close voice. Remember, a shift in p.o.v. from third to first is not just changing the pronoun references; it's an entirely different way of seeing the same scene.

Third distant is omniscient, a voice outside the story that has created this fictional world.

First distant is a character recalling events that happened to him/her. They exist solely in their fictional world.

Third distant is objectively aware.

First distant is as objective as possible but because it's the voice of a fallible human being, it's subjective by nature.

DIALOG

My idea of dealing with dialog at this point, after characterization, point of view and setting, is that dialog really only works well when you know who your characters are, where they are and what they're doing. Starting out with dialog is focusing artificially on what they say because it's out of the context of your story.

Dialog in fiction is not like conversation in real life, because dialog in fiction is part of intensified reality, and let's be honest, most conversation in real life is boring and pointless. Dialog does, however, have to 'sound' real to the reader, but understand something; dialog in fiction is on the page, it is written, not heard, which means you have to be very aware of punctuation, rhythms, vocabulary and syntax. You also have to set dialog up because it depends upon its impact for the context within which it occurs. Dialog is also a very fast way of moving a story forward, and a very painless way for the reader to receive information. But before we get into all that, we need to know the traditional dialog format.

The standard form for dialog is to paragraph after every line of dialog, no matter how short. For example, from my short story "Elvis Is Missing":

"I heard she seen Elvis last week over at the Burger King in Dismal Seepage."

"Yep. Like to fainted too."

"Well..."

No matter how short the line, even one word, you paragraph. Also standard is the use of quotation marks to open and close the actual line of dialog. If you decide you want to do away with quotation marks, you should do so for a good reason, not just for the hell of it. Some writers feel the least amount of punctuation possible, including quotation marks, is good. Cormac McCarthy is an excellent example of this. The one thing to always keep in mind, is to not confuse your reader. If that happens with the removal of quotation marks, then it's a mistake.

Another technique used in a dialog scene is to shift from a line of dialog to a descriptive line coming from the distant voice, then back to dialog, like this from my novella, Last Trip to Truchas:

"Very easy now or I'll drain your sinus cavities, permanently."

His eyes were wide, his mouth open and his gun hand pinned to the floor with the suddenness of his fall.

"Okay, in slo-mo, lift the hand with the gun, leaving the gun on the floor. Excellent." I stepped closer and kicked the pistol across the floor, well away from him, then I stepped back and looked around the cabin.

The point here is that if you don't paragraph at the non dialog line, and put it immediately following the line of dialog, the reader might misunderstand who spoke that first line because it has no identity tag. Always paragraph when you shift from character to character in a dialog scene, even if the character doesn't say anything but you're describing a reaction. Readers understand that when you paragraph you're shifting the focus to another character. That's part of the basic format of dialog, and if you consistently violate that, it is a major mistake. Let me reemphasize this point: readers are accustomed to certain techniques and if you violate those techniques inconsistently, you're going to lose the reader. And if you deliberately ignore an established technique, such as paragraphing in dialog, you should be going for something new that enhances the story. There's got to be a reason for violating any of the standard formats readers are taught to expect.

You've no doubt noticed in the three sample lines of dialog about Elvis, there were no basic identifying tags, which is another basic in the dialog format, as in the following example with the tags underlined:

"Az-tec jools," Rudy said.

Old Ralph stared at him. "Whut?"

An identifying tag does just what it says, it identifies the speaker. This is the simplest form of separating speakers there is, and the reader becomes so used to tags such as the ones above, or the 'he said,' 'she said,' tags, they don't really notice them, just like they don't notice punctuation if it's used correctly. If it's not, you're in trouble. Also note that the identifying tag can come after, before or even during the line of dialog, like this:

"Az-tec," Rudy paused dramatically, "jools."

Varying the placement of identifying tags in a dialog keeps it from becoming boring or repetitive, but if you overdo it, it becomes self parody.

Another point arises in this example; in the actual line of dialog, I use the phonetic spelling of jewels, i.e., 'jools', and take the chance that the reader will understand what is meant. If this were the only example of phonetic spelling in the dialog, it wouldn't work, but because this is a consistent within the dialog of these characters, I can assume that most readers will figure it out.

The next step up from a basic identification tag is business. Business is something the writer or narrator describes outside the actual dialog lines that deals with actions, settings, reactions, gestures, etcetera. Business can precede or follow a line of dialog or interrupt the dialog to describe something in the scene. As in the following examples taken from my collection of short stories, The Holy City Zoo:

Preceding the dialog:

Woody leaned his elbows on the bar and squinted at him. "Elvis? In the Burger King?"

Following the dialog:

"Yep. Just settin' there eatin' a Whopper." Rudy studied the Olympic circles he'd made on the bar with the bottom of his beer glass.

Interrupting the dialog:

"I'll be damned," Woody straightened up, his eyes wide, like a thought had just come to him. "I'll bet Elvis'd like to meet Pussytoes."

You don't want to overdo business in a dialog scene but it is a very handy and quick way to let the reader see gestures, expressions, movement and even setting, as in the following example from my short story, "The Bird's Graveyard" in The Holy City Zoo collection:

"Where you reckon birds go to die?" Old Ralph sets his Coors down real careful on the bar like he's afraid a quick move might spook Woody, and then turns his head super slow an' looks at him, his eyes all squinty. "Whut?"

"Birds," Woody says, "Where you reckon they go to die?"

Old Ralph studies him like he's looking at a new kinda bug that'd just crawled up on that bar stool. He shakes his head and looks at Mister Hoover.

"Don't he ask the damnedest questions, Mister Hoover?"

"Where do they?" Mister Hoover says, always tryin' to keep Old Ralph off balance.

"Well damnit," Old Ralph says, "they don't go nowhere. They just die, that's all."

Woody finishes off his Coors, rips off a burp, and shakes his head. "I ain't never seen a bird that died of old age, have you?"

Old Ralph sighs and looks around the Holy City Bar and Mineral Water Baths like someone'd just accused him of abusin' a goat. "How in hell can you tell if a bird's died of old age?"

"Well sir," Woody says, " I seen 'em shot, and I seen 'em hit by trucks, and I seen 'em got by dogs and such, but I ain't never come across one just plain old dead. Have you?"

"Ah hell..." Old Ralph stops, blinks, then looks over at Mister

Hoover again. "By god Mister Hoover, I believe Woody's right. I never seen a bird just dead of natural causes, have you?"

"Old Ralph, I haven't made a study of dead birds."

This confession of ignorance don't surprise Old Ralph or anyone else in the bar. Mister Hoover's an ex college professor, and was a livin' demonstration of Why Our Schools Have Failed.

CROSS REFERENCE:
ESTABLISHING RHYTHMS II

There is one unusual point about this preceding dialog scene; the narrator that describes the actions, gestures, etcetera, is a character in the scene, which is evident through his grammar and syntax, but everything this narrator reports to the reader is clear enough so the reader gets the atmosphere of the dialog. And it is all external, no thoughts or feelings.

In the dialog business, it's clearly established that this scene takes place in a bar, [underlined] and in a later bit of dialog business, the bar is identified as 'The Holy City Bar and Mineral Water Baths.' [underlined]

In the last line of the scene, [underlined] the narrator gives some biographical background on one of the characters in the scene. Since there are three characters in the scene, identifying tags are necessary, but to just identify them would destroy the tone and flow of the scene, which is why the narrator, who provides the tags and business, is one of the characters. If this were a third person distant narrator, the number and length of the interruptions would be intrusive, but because the narrator is a character in the scene, his observations are not intrusive. This use of a character as the narrator was done to make the business more than just clarification of the scene; it's establishing another voice, another character and he reveals himself in the way he describes the dialog. This use of a character-narrator is also an example of showing rather than telling.

This example of a standard third person distant narrator, is from my novel, The Ghost Dancers, Book II:

"Uh, Jim," Toby consciously controlled his reaction. "Are you sure about

how the bodies looked? I mean are you sure there was no mark of violence?"

"Sure as I'm sittin' here."

"Know what I think?" Another man spoke up. "I think it was one of them Northers we been hearin' about. They can do that, you know."

"They could, but they wouldn't." Toby spoke angrily, realizing instantly he'd said more than he should. The only person he had even discussed the Ghost Dancers with was Kate in an effort to learn what she and others thought about the Dancers. He made certain she had no idea he was one of them.

The group stared at him.

Reynolds cleared his throat. "Well, now just how sure are you, Toby? I mean how do you know they wouldn't?"

"I just know, that's all. Hell, I've been all over the North for the past six or seven years. I'd know if they'd done something like that."

"I don't believe they really exist, anyway," another man spoke. "Just a lot of spook stories."

"Yeah," Toby said, "you're right, it's probably nothing."

Dirk, a recluse who lived up near the old radar station, squinted at Toby through a wild, dirty tangle of black hair that seemed to be intertwining with his equally wild and dirty tangle of beard. It was like seeing a pair of emotionless lizard eyes peering out from a hairy bush. He grinned, revealing green scummed teeth.

"I'll bet them dudes was killed by what I seen the other night."

Identifying the focus character is critical if you have several speakers in a dialog scene. Without a focus character, the dialog will have no point and seem random. Even in a dialog scene with two characters, one has to be a focus character.

In the preceding scene, several of the speakers are not specifically identified, as in the second line of dialog, [underlined] where there is no identity tag, and the following line where the speaker is simply identified as 'Another man.' [underlined] In a scene like this, when a speaker is specifically identified, it sets him up as being more significant. 'Reynolds" is an example of that, because his reaction to Toby is significant later in the book. And in the last paragraph, Dirk is not only given a specific identity tag, he is described by the distant voice, which sets him out as the most significant character in the scene after the focus character.

Another point about dialog; in the third person voice, it is clear that within the quotation marks, the reader is 'hearing' what the characters say, which is close voice, but it's not always clear if the voice identifying the speakers and reporting the 'business' of the scene is distant or close. The way to make that clear is to identify immediately that this is a character narrating the business, and through the style of the voice narrating the dialog scene. For example, this is a close voice narrating a dialog scene:

Hoover grinned. He knew that Old Ralph knew the odds were a thousand to one that Virgil was pullin' him in on another scam, but the man jus' couldn't back off from a treasure hunt. Never could.

The opening line identifies Hoover as the focus here, and the next line shifts to the personal pronoun 'he' so that it could be close voice, and then in that line there is a vocabulary shift to the vernacular with the word pullin', which makes it definitely the close voice as well as 'jus'. Then, the last line of two words, 'Never could,' reemphasizes the close voice style. To make this a third distant voice you remove the close voice references by changing the vocabulary and syntax:

Hoover smiled to himself because he knew Old Ralph was aware that the odds were a thousand to one that Virgil was pulling him in on another scam, but Old Ralph couldn't back away from a treasure hunt. He was simply incapable.

To continue the example of using the third person close voice in dialog:

Old Ralph looked at Virgil, all squinty eyed. "Hows come you ain't got that treasure you own self?"

Virgil shrugged one shoulder under this Clint Eastwood poncho he'd taken to wearin' after watchin' a week of spaghetti westerns on the the teevee. "It's heavy, esay, I need some help."

The phrase, 'all squinty eyed' is in the vernacular, and is obviously close voice rather than the more proper distant voice which would describe the same thing as, 'Old Ralph squinted at Virgil.' Also the phrase, 'this Clint Eastwood poncho' is also a close voice phrasing due primarily to the word, 'this' which expresses an attitude about the poncho. Changing the article to 'a' changes the impact of the line, i.e., 'a Clint Eastwood poncho.' Also the dropping of the 'g' in the 'ing' endings is indicative of the close voice.

One final point about use of business in dialog. How many times have you been reading a book and a line of dialog is given, then followed by a piece of business like, 'she screeched.' This means you have to go back and re-read the line or re-evaluate the impact because the business was out of place, i.e., there was no indication of how the line was delivered by the character. The result of such a line is that the reader is jerked out of the reality of the story for a moment and the scene is destroyed. It's just poor writing. Move your tags and business to where they will be most effective.

Giving the character's dialog a personal style is tricky. Characters can and do use a vernacular of their own, but if you overdo it, it becomes self parody. You have to find ways of giving the dialog just a touch here and there. Dropping the 'g' in 'ing' endings for example, but not always doing that, or dropping another ending, like 'mus' instead of must. What you try to do is use the rhythms of actual speech, the music of the language, but you intensify it.

One thing I do that I find invaluable in recreating speech rhythms, is to read my rough draft into a tape recorder, exactly the way I've written it, punctuation and all, then I listen to the tape as I follow it on *the page* and edit the manuscript. You'll hear things you would never pick up in just writing it and reading it to yourself.

THE FOUR POINT PLOT LINE

Now that we have characters moving around in a setting and talking to one another, it's time to give them purpose, otherwise known as a plot line. Of all the formats for plot that I've seen and heard, the simplest and most adaptable is the four point plot line:

CONFLICT
COMPLICATION
CRISIS
CONCLUSION

CONFLICT: The first element in any plot has to be conflict, but we have to be very careful how we define conflict. In the most general sense, conflict is the driving force behind a story, the idea or event or situation the writer wants to explore, which implies the discovery of something new. This could mean several things but most often it means the writer is coming to the subject to discover what it reveals about the human condition. It can also mean the author sees something in the culture that h/she thinks is worth exploring or revealing. In other words, the conflict in fiction is first of all, whatever drives the writer to write that story.

On a much more concrete-intellectual level, there are the academic/ literary versions of conflict:

Character vs Character: this is the most basic conflict of all, which is individuals clashing with one another. The clash is most often physical in nature, but you rarely find a pure character vs character conflict because it doesn't offer much in the way of complications. There's always something else involved which leads to the following conflicts:

Character vs Nature: here you have stories of climbers on mountains, explorers in unknown territory, sailing alone around the world, etcetera, all are within this conflict, but again, it's never that simple. A combination of character vs nature also involves,

Character vs Self: here the central character has to face fears, doubts, weaknesses, strengths, etcetera, in order to overcome the basic conflict, which might be the previous one, character vs nature. The character vs self conflict usually involves one or more of the other basic conflicts.

Character vs The Divine: in the modern sense this conflict would be more likely symbolic than actual, it all depends upon your character and what the thematic conflict is. More often in modern times this conflict can be expressed as being ***Character vs Culture:*** These conflicts are fine for interpretation of literature but they're just too cosmic for use in creating a story. The writer is faced with reducing such literary conflicts down to its essence in order to determine what the most basic conflict is. It's easier if you already have a story idea and you're trying to make sense of it as a piece of fiction.

For example, I took this quote from a newspaper article: *"High tech entrepreneurs have ideas for education reform – and the money to try them." I wondered, what would high tech innovations in the high school lead to, given a particular cultural attitude and what basic conflict would appear? The most logical is character vs character, but what characters? A traditional teacher vs a high tech, computer oriented teacher? The focus is clearer now, and within that conflict you might discover another conflict, a sub-plot like character vs culture, or character vs self. You can continue this reductio ad absurdum exercise forever, but what will happen with this reduction exercise, is that if you understand what the basic conflict is, then you're going to be able to sort out the relevant sub-plots from the interesting but non useable side trips."*

Although I've separated these basic conflicts they are not unconnected to characterization and setting. As an example I'll use the general story idea from The Touchmaster's Network. The idea I was interested in exploring was the degree of responsibility a teacher has for how students carry out what he has taught them both as a teacher and as a role model. I set the story in the near future, in a culture that is becoming more and more restrictive due to fear of attacks from terrorists, other countries and from within. But, to continue the ideal of a democracy, and to control inevitable adolescent rebellion, each school is assigned a "Designated Dissident," a teacher whom the school board and administrators know is the official dissident, the one through whom the students can express their rebellion. However, none of the faculty nor any of the students and parents, know who the Designated Dissident actually Is in order to give the position more credibility. It is a position of great trust.

I also wanted to take advantage of the quantum leaps in medical technology. Ultimately I put the central character, a teacher who is the Designated Dissident, in a situation where he has to agree to help a student of his going into a very dangerous situation in order to uncover a real 'subversive' organization. The conflict is made very personal for the teacher because the student, a teenage girl, has an electronic implant that sends visual and oral information back to a central location where the teacher is monitoring her experiences. The teacher, who has filled her with idealism, now has to follow her, via the monitor, as she moves deeper into danger. The student believes in what she is doing because the teacher has encouraged her, and as she gets more involved, so does the teacher. This is a thematic conflict.

CROSS REFERENCE:
ABSURDITY AS THEME; THE ROSE NOTES
BANALITY OF EVIL; THE ROSE NOTES

At this point I have to think about setting, which now means something very general, like the time of the story, past, present or future. Because I recognize that hyperbole is a basic tool of the fiction writer, and that intensified reality is what gives fiction that fourth dimension, this almost automatically rejects the present as an acceptable time span because readers would be much more likely to reject any hyperbole in the story. The past is a possibility, but because that would also require too much justification for altering reality, the near future seems to hold the most promise.

The question now is, how far in the future. Because I want to make a relevant comment on events happening now, that moves the future setting to something very near, say one or two decades. This near future setting allows me to use present day situations with just a few leaps in technology, like the implanting of biotrodes, and intensifying the terrorist paranoia of the people and the government.

Now I have to figure out how to introduce the central character into a situation that hasn't existed in his/her life before. I already have a general idea of the setting, i.e., an increasingly paranoid culture, becoming more restrictive due to real and imagined threats, and I add that factor to how a public school would reflect that cultural atmosphere. For example, here is a classroom setting from The Touchmaster's Network:

The stations quickly filled and students busily entered their handprint i.d. on the individual CRTs at each station, automatically recording attendance in the central office. They repeated this in each class which kept them located throughout the day. Any movement outside the classroom was also recorded, whether it be the rest room, the library or the quad for lunch. Any deviation in the time schedule of any student was immediately noted in the central office and tracked down by school security. It was virtually impossible to lose track of a student for more than a few minutes. Every student was taught from kindergarten on, that THE AUTHORITIES knew where they were and what they were doing every moment of every day. Obedience assured survival.

Now, going back to the original basic conflict, a teacher's responsibility to students, and from there, and with the help of this general setting, I begin to clarify the complications.

COMPLICATION: A complication should test a different aspect of your central character's personality, and/or present a different side of the basic conflict. Because I have a fairly complex conflict, [teacher's responsibility to students] the possibilities of complications appear infinite, but with the cultural setting I've set up, the complications begin to focus more clearly, and with the nature of the central character's personality the complications will become more evident.

At this point I have to seriously consider the character, who he/she is and what kind of person they are, which I already know in a general way at this point, and it's now that I should consider the fine details of this character that will effect the plot line. I already know the character is very intelligent, teaches English, and is idealistic, which usually means in conflict with the culture. In this case, however, the character begins as an idealist who believes in what the culture is doing, and accepts the position of Designated Dissident in order to support the culture's goals. As he continues in his role of Designated Dissident, he begins to believe more and more in the causes he is supposed to pretend to believe in, and thus begin the complications.

At his point my view of teaching becomes critical in how I develop this character. I think teaching is one of the most difficult and misunderstood professions in existence. I also believe that a good teacher is very rare and has qualities of integrity, intelligence, morality and ethical responsibility that very few people in the culture have.

These are the qualities I want my character to have, but, not as a paragon.

The character's gender is important here, not just in terms of knowing who they are, but in terms of how they face conflict and how they are thought of by the culture. I made the character male, for various reasons, but dominant among them is the fact that I think the American culture considers teaching to be a female job and thus the dominant male attitude toward male teachers is condescending. And an English teacher is even more of a male outcast. This is a sub text that will add texture to the basic story line. These are the things that give a piece of fiction depth.

In *The Touchmaster's Network,* I know I'm going to have a series of complications because the conflict for a novel has to be fairly complex. This means I'm going to use the full complexity of the characterization as the story progresses. The complications to the basic conflict will test many strengths and weaknesses of the character and now I have to think of structure, i.e., how will I order the complications so that they will increase in drama and lead inevitably toward the ultimate complication the character must resolve. There has to be a logical movement from one complication to the next, and that movement has to be tied to the conflict and finally to the climax of the story.

The first complication in *The Touchmaster's Network,* is that the central character, the teacher, begins to believe in what he professes to believe, that is in the ideals and goals of the Touchmaster's Network. In general, there should be a direct line from the conflict, through the complications, to the crisis-conclusion. This line may not be evident to the reader, but it needs to be clear to the writer and for one very important reason; the writer has to know how the conflict is resolved in relation to the central character, that is, does s/he win or lose? This vital point, determined at the beginning of the story or novel, gives the story narrative pull, without which the story will tend to lose focus. If the writer doesn't know what the win or lose ending is, and hopes to discover what it is during the writing, the story will reflect that in the way the plot line wanders into dead ends, strays from the main point and finally hits on it and moves quickly to the conclusion. And that is a lot of rewriting.

The point here is simple: you gain control of your story line by knowing, generally, how the story ends. This doesn't mean you know how, or where, or when or any of the specifics of the ending, you just know the most critical element; the central character wins or loses, lives or dies. And clearly, if you're in first person, your character has to live to tell the story, but s/he can still win or lose.

In a short story, the conflict would be very basic, very straightforward, because there isn't enough time to develop complexities. The conflict in a short story would be selected to set up a minimum of two complications. One complication is too simple, because it doesn't really show that much about the character. This means I'm probably going to test just two aspects of the character's personality, say physical courage and the strength of beliefs. Of those two, I have to determine which is the most significant for the story and if it's strength of beliefs, I make that the last complication he/she is faced with and resolves, or doesn't, depending upon intent for the story.

One great thing about approaching plot this way, is that if you have a well developed character, you're going to discover new complications to the basic conflict that are even more revealing of his/her personality, as you write the story.

CRISIS-CONCLUSION: To give the story rising action to the conclusion, you need to make each complication more difficult than the previous one and also different. A series of physical complications the central character must resolve, simply become hurdles over which he or she jumps, not a real testing of who they are. This means knowing the characters strengths or weaknesses well enough so that you can reveal the character to a reader through the resolution of the complications. But above all else, you have to know before you write the story, how it ends, that is, does the central character win or lose? Knowing this gives your story narrative pull.

Here is a breakdown of the conflict, complications and crisis-conclusion for *The Touchmaster's Network:*

CONFLICT: a teacher's moral/ethical responsibility to his students

COMPLICATION 1: he is suddenly offered the chance to back up what he says in class as the 'Designated Dissident' about challenging authority, by joining an underground group, The Touchmaster's Network, that has been placed on the attorney general's list of terrorist organizations.

COMPLICATION 2: as a member of The Touchmaster's Network, he is asked to recruit students into the group. At the same time, he is required to take a group of students to a public execution as part of his teaching duties. It turns out the condemned person is a student of his who was picked up by the Home Security Committee for belonging to *The Touchmaster's Network.*

COMPLICATION 3: A female student of his is asked by *The Touchmaster's Network* to investigate rumors of a concentration camp being set up for homeless people, several hundred miles south of the Bay Area. She is surgically implanted with a biotrode that broadcasts visual and audio data back to a central point, where the teacher is asked to monitor her progress and pass the data along.

COMPLICATION 4: the female student's biotrode suddenly stops broadcasting.

COMPLICATION 5: the teacher is sent to the concentration camp to find her and/or to bring back the information she was gathering.

COMPLICATION 6: a former male student of the teacher's appears in camp as a member of the military unit guarding the camp, and stumbles across a secret group called *The Shining Path*, within the camp that is an offshoot of *The Touchmaster's Network,* and threatens to reveal them. In order to prove his loyalty to Shining Path, the teacher is asked to kill the former student by the secret group in the camp, both as a necessity and as a test of his loyalty to the *Touchmaster's Network.*

COMPLICATION 7: the black plague breaks out in the camp, which is subsequently abandoned by the guards, and the inmates escape, carrying the plague out into the surrounding area. The female student is still alive and moving north as well, and she is carrier of the plague.

COMPLICATION 8: the teacher joins *Shining Path* in their escape from the camp as they move north, toward his home, carrying the plague with them. They discover a 'plague line' has been set up to the north, south and east of the camp. Anyone attempting to cross the line is killed.

CRISIS – CONCLUSION: He arrives home to find his friends in *The Touchmaster's Network* have been betrayed, some of them killed, some of them imprisoned for questioning. He doesn't know if anyone has named him as a member yet. Of the original group he and his female student are the only ones left in that area, and she betrays him to save her life.

Does he continue or not?

I have to know what the conclusion is before I write the story, that is, does he go on or not. There are several things to consider here, but most importantly it's what point I want to make with this story, i.e., how should a teacher 'see' his students, that is are they less important as individuals and more important as members of a group fighting for an ideal? It's not a matter of his own physical courage here, it's the depth of his beliefs. I'm still making a point about teachers and students here, so that has to be a major consideration in how I end the novel.

The Rose Notes

A word of explanation: The "Rose Notes" began several years ago during my participation on a writers' board sponsored by AOL. During the initial stages of that board, we were discussing point of view, and a debate arose about how valid a character of a gender opposite the author, can be. My position was that gender didn't matter when you're an author, characterization was everything.

In support of that I cited a story of mine entitled "Rose" in which the central character was a young girl. The story was accepted by a woman's magazine and I received a note from the editor who said they loved the story and 'knew' that it was autobiographical and very moving. From that point on I signed my posts on the writer's board with 'Rose.'

Several months went by, and the original few on the board grew to many, and none of the new posters knew who Rose was. They assumed I was a woman, and the women on the board began to e-mail me and discuss topics from the board, personally. I responded as I would with anyone. A few more months passed and I revealed to the writers on the board that I was in fact a man. The other men were bemused. The women were outraged. I had betrayed them. I had pretended to be a woman and they had 'confided' in me. I replied that there was nothing deceptive except the name Rose. I answered them as a human being and a writer. Gender was irrelevant. Except to many of the women. To this day I have no idea what that means.

Anyway, 'The Rose Note's are discussions we had on that board, and other discussions on writing I've had over the internet and in my workshops . I preface some of the discussions with an explanation of how it came about.

Point of View Shifts

[This is a response to a question about point of view in the novel Martha Peake by McGrath from a friend of mine and a fellow writer, who has been in my Asilomar Workshop for many years.]

Q: Does McGrath use the same point of view shifts as James Lee Burke?

No, not really. James Lee Burke just writes himself into a corner with his first person p.o.v. and shifts to a distant voice, claiming it's close, but clearly it can't be because in those sections he does that he gets into the mind of the characters, the character is talking about. Burke usually covers himself at the beginning of these sections by having his character say something like, "Well, I wasn't there but this is what I was told happened," and then the character goes on in a clearly third person omniscient point of view, i.e. telling the reader what the secondary character's emotions, thoughts and impressions were. If Burke did that throughout his novel, it would be a reasonable p.o.v. shift, but he only does it when he gets stuck and has to give the reader information that his first person narrator can't relate. This just shows you that even the best selling writers still have technique problems.

Martha Peake begins with a narrator, the nephew, relating a story about a woman told to him by his uncle. The thing here, is that the narrator even admits to the reader that he's unreliable, but he is closer to the 'truth' than his uncle. It's a nice distinction here between truth and reality. Another thing that's interesting is that the reader's reaction to the narrator becomes more sympathetic, more positive as the narrator becomes more unreliable. His unreliability is his growth from curiosity to admiration to love for this woman. At times McGrath[the author] does the same thing Burke does, i.e., simply abandons the first person distant narrator and goes right into the close voice, and not just with the central character, but with secondary characters as well. The only thing that makes this consistent is that when the narrator does that, it's always within the context of the story *of Martha Peake.*

Moral: you can get away with anything if it works.

Practically yours, Rose

Absurdity As A Theme

Q: Why is it we seem to be more concerned with how people see themselves rather than how we write about these people?

I too have wondered about the way we've been going here, but I know that for myself I've gone into a lurk and leap mode. I am now in the leap mode. Here goes…

Reading the messages here in the past few weeks has made me think of a particular subject that serious writers, no matter what their genre, are dealing with, which is the increasing absurdity of our lives. Let me define absurdity: it is that state in which the setting of your life disintegrates and you are left with the essence of what you are, the core of your being. (I'm trying to develop a literary counterpart of the chaos theory for myself. I'll let you know how it works out. If it's not too chaotic.)

One great horror for modern individuals is that when you peel away all the layers of identity your culture has given you, and get down to your core, there may be no essence there, and the only alternatives left are:

1) to rebuild an identity in much the same way as it was constructed in the first place, and so repeat all the mistakes that led us to collapse, or

2) attempt to rebuild our identity so that we become 'authentic', or

3) the final alternative, die.

The second choice is the rare one, one that is hard for a materialistic culture to deal with in that authenticity means becoming basically human, or creative. The first alternative is the modern version of tragedy. The second may also be tragic but with comic overtones. The third is tragic reality. I find myself more and more writing about the third alternative. In the Hemingway tradition, it's not if you die, it's how.

In my mind, those three alternatives constitute basic plot lines.

Which leads me to irony. I find myself, as the author, resorting to irony more as a defense against the inauthentic human actions in the world, but for me it becomes an aggressive defense, and I think it takes away from the work. It's very difficult to separate your life persona from your writing persona, and I'm not even sure we should. It's just something else that you have to be aware of and control.

However, if I give that ironic tendency to a character, I understand it more clearly, where it comes from, what its target really is, etc. Instead of a blunt instrument, it becomes a scalpel. (I don't care to carry that analogy out any further.) In any case, I think writers in general may tend toward irony more than most folks because they are more concerned with the human condition and are more moved by it. Irony becomes our shield and sword but I think vulnerability is a more effective stance for the writer.

One final (I promise!) note. I realized recently that every time I create strong characters, a good part of me goes into them, and eventually, if I'm not constantly rebuilding myself through experience, I'll run out of parts. I've become a literary chop shop!!

Absurdly yours, Rose

Technique Overload

I just finished reading Annie Proulx's new book *Accordion Crimes* and I have to say I'm disappointed after *The Shipping News*, but for reasons of writing techniques she used. For example, like *Postcards,* this is episodic, and I'm not sure why she selected that structure for this subject. It never seemed to work for me for several reasons. For example, within an episode, she would shift into a narrative voice set off by parentheses and summarize the rest of the character's life to his or her death, effectively cutting that story line off.

Also, within too many of the episodes, she used the catalogue in what was apparently intended to be an intense summary of whatever was going on at the time. It worked in a few places but once it began to appear with great regularity, I found myself scanning, not really that interested in another catalogue, particularly from the narrator. A character's catalogue might have worked on occasion.

I thought the hiding of the one thousand dollar bills in the accordion was a very artificial device used to keep the reader interested. Eventually you just don't care, and the ending, although ironic, just didn't work as a justification for using the accordion as the tying object.

It was clear from the start that she was writing with great irony as the dominant tone, an examination of bigotry from all sides, which again was effective up to a point, then it simply became repetitive and predictable.

I was kept involved in the novel because of her writing, the brilliant use of simile, her descriptions, and occasionally, some really wild humor. For example, after describing a tragic and depressing scene in a hospital emergency room, the last sentence says, "The room smelled of guinea pigs." This was not connected to anything in the scene and was so bizarre all you could do was laugh.

I'm curious about what her intent was, that is, what did she want the book to elicit from a reader? My reaction at the end, was, so what? I wasn't surprised or enraged at the various forms of bigotry she described. It simply confirmed, yet again, something I already knew, but gave me no new insights into this question.

One thing I did like: her choice of the accordion as the instrument. I saw that as humorously ironic because there are too many people who are 'prejudiced' against that kind of music. But I'm also not certain if the accordion isn't a cliché similar to bowling as a class distinction.

Pick-ily yours, Rose

The Banality of Evil

[Q: This is in response to a question about how villains in fiction are drawn, and what is the most effective portrayal.]

On the banality of evil. I think we all expect evil to be horrific, easily recognizable and thus abhorrent to all reasoning people, and clearly it isn't, which may explain why evil is so omnipresent in our culture. We seem to believe that evil is physically ugly, and clearly repugnant, but that's not the way it usually works. In most cases, this is the view of evil that is presented on TV. and in the movies.

Further, we expect evil to be expressed in a single, intense act such as rape, murder, molestation, war atrocities, etc, and most often it isn't. In fact, those acts are simply the end result of many small expressions of evil that accumulated until the explosion took place. We are a culture who treats symptoms rather than the disease.

In this morning's local paper there was a photograph of a woman holding a picket sign that read STOP IMMIGRATION + ILLEGALS, STOP GIVING AMERICAN JOBS AWAY. She wears what looks like an American flag over her shoulders. Her mouth is twisted downward in a grimace of anger and hatred. Somebody's mother, and probably grandmother. She has found her evil, the focus for everything gone wrong with her view of what life should be. And aliens caused it all.

I walk a half block away from my house to an onion field. I see thirty or forty Mexican farm laborers out there hoeing weeds in an onion field, the target of the woman's hatred. A half mile away I see fifty or more Mexican farm laborers harvesting lettuce. It's amazing how few white middle class people are out there in the fields, unless they own them. It's amazing how few white people of any economic class are out there. It's amazing that 90% of the field labor done in California is done by Mexican laborers. The same men and women I see every Friday in the post office, sending money orders home to their families, not drinking, buying drugs, etc. etc.

I see the face of evil in that white, middle class woman, wrapped in the flag, blaming people she doesn't know for her problems that she barely understands.

It is evil to allow anyone, adults or children, to live in p.o.v.erty when there are individuals and corporations making obscene profits. The small, daily insults to humanity caused by p.o.v.erty ultimately result in the single, intense explosion that culture condemns; rape, murder, molestation, but there is no blame attached to the cause of this evil.

It is evil to declare 'war' on p.o.v.erty, drugs, illiteracy, etc etc ad infinitum, ad absurdum, but never intend to actually put the country on an actual war footing, that is, to dedicate the entire effort of the government to eradicating that named enemy. All that has resulted from the many declared pseudo wars has been an eroding of confidence in our government and in the elected officials.

It is evil that voting has become a negative act in which people don't vote for, they vote against.

It is evil what we have allowed to happen to our educational system.

It is evil to pass laws with no intention of enforcing them or obeying them. I give you the 55 mph speed limit, and now the 65 mph speed limit, litter laws, car pool only lanes, parking restrictions, etc etc etc.

It is evil to hear someone use a racial epithet and say nothing to them.

It is evil that we have become so tolerant of negativity that we allow vicious, hate spewing talk show hosts to become popular.

It is evil that we allow gratuitous violence to be the mainstay of entertainment.

To quote Pogo: I have met the enemy and he is us.

Depressingly yours, Rose

Establishing Rhythms

[Q: You spoke of establishing rhythms in prose. Could you explain that?]

Here's an attempt to show what I was talking about in terms of establishing rhythm in prose. This is taken from a work in progress entitled The Ceremony of Innocence.*[the title taken from Yeats' poem]*

[this is the original prose piece]

That gray bearded, granite eyed, Scot Presbyterian bigot, barely tolerating the community of the wagon train until he could leave it, which he did, in the Colorado Territory at the first sight of the blue-black mountains rising on the western horizon, a relief after endless days through an ocean of beige colored grass on the flat prairie of Kansas and Eastern Colorado, walking quickly to the lead ox, turning it toward the jagged peaks, pulling his wagon out of line, ignoring the shouts of the wagon master, the warnings, striding out ahead of his wife and son in the ox-drawn wagon, his rifle held firmly in his right hand, ready for use against the Utes, white prospectors, trappers, bear, deer, rabbits, mountain lions, any damnable thing that either *helped or* hindered his progress toward the spot he had already named in his Old Testament mind, Bered, 'a place in the wilderness,' where he, Elijah Robertson would establish the American branch of the Highland Robertson clan. Which he did. With a vengeance.

[Now here I break it up into 8-12 syllable lines]

That gray bearded, granite eyed, Scot
Presbyterian bigot, barely
tolerating the community of the
wagon train until he could leave it, which he did,

in the Colorado Territory at the
first sight of the blue-black mountains rising on the
western horizon, a relief after endless
days through an ocean of beige colored grass on the
flat prairie of Kansas and Eastern
Colorado, walking quickly to the lead ox,
turning it toward the jagged peaks, pulling his
wagon out of line, ignoring the shouts of the
wagon master, the warnings, striding out ahead
of his wife and son in the ox-drawn wagon, his
rifle held firmly in his right hand, ready for
use against the Utes, white prospectors, trappers, bear,
deer, rabbits, mountain lions,any damnable
thing that either helped or hindered his progress toward
the spot he had already named in his Old
Testament mind, Bered, 'a place in the
wilderness,' where he, Elijah Robertson would
establish the American branch of the
Highland Robertson clan. Which he did. With a
vengeance.

I wanted to change the origin of the passage from third person distant narrator to third person close, character. The first thing I notice about the prose passage is the number of 3+ syllable words I used to get the flow I wanted, the movement to parallel the movement of the character. At the time of writing and rewriting that, I was consciously thinking of the rhythms of movement and each time I rewrote a line or more, I would read it aloud to hear how it sounded and how it "felt on the tongue," which basically means I wanted the passage to be able to be read aloud and gain in power, like poetry.

The next step is to go through the broken lines passage and begin to smooth it out. Here it's impossible to show you the various permutations I try to get a line right, I take words out, put in new ones, moving them around, check the syllable length, over and over until the line flows. I also begin to look for striking alliterations, dissonance, word pairs, power verbs, etc that add depth to each line. One thing begins to happen frequently here…words like 'the' begin to disappear with great regularity, giving me one more syllable to use more effectively. I also discovered ideas or emotions that should have been in the lines but weren't.

Grandfather Elijah gray bearded, granite eyed,	*[repeat of the g sound]*
a Scot Presbyterian bigot, barely	
tolerating the wagon train community	
straining to leave it, to strike out alone,	*[the s sound repeated deliberately]*
stunned in Colorado Territory at his	
first sight of blue-black mountains rising ragged	*[alliteration worked for here]*
on the western horizon, blessed relief	
after endless days on the beige grass ocean	*[working for economy of language]*
prairie of Kansas and Eastern Colorado,	
he strode to the lead ox, yanked it toward the jagged	*[here I worked for a more abrupt rhythm of action]*
peaks, drove his wagon out of line, deaf to	
the wagon master's warnings, striding away,	*[here I discovered I wanted to give a sense of helplessness to these characters]*
wife and son in the ox-drawn wagon swept along	
wide eyed, clinging, throwing longing glances	
at the fading figures fixed motionless behind.	*[alliteration again]*
Ox whip in his left hand, rifle in his right, ready	
for Crow raiding parties, drunken trappers, outlaws,	*[details here to enhance the aura of the west]*
bear, cougars, deer, elk, any damnable thing that	
helped or hindered his progress toward that single site,	
silently named in his Old Testament mind,	
Bered, 'a place in the wilderness,' where he	
resettled the Highland clan. With a	
vengeance.	

The passage has now shifted from being a third person distant (narrator) which is informational, to a third person close(character) which now becomes a part of the character's psyche, it's his recollection of his family's history, not information about them given by the narrative voice. I want the character to have this depth of ancestral knowledge, to have it in him with as much reality as day to day living. I wanted these ancestral memories to be intensified, to give them a quality apart from the immediate present state of the character's mind. To me, the intense sense of place and of roots, are both critical in the novel.

The central character is an eco-terrorist who comes home to find his family's land threatened by developers. In order for the reader to understand and accept his actions, they have to feel his emotional depth of devotion to the land and his family. This particular memory comes to the central character, Mattathias, as he travels by train closer to his home in Colorado.

The problem was though, that it still was too heavy in 'word density' in the paragraph form, for it to have the reader to be aware of each separate thought, and in a normal paragraph that doesn't happen. I now have a structural decision, i.e., stay with the standard prose paragraph or go with the more poetic format. I decided to go with the poetic format, for the reason stated.

What I want to do is clearly separate the third person distant narrative voice from the third person close character voice and to me the most effective way to do that is to change the style. I don't use this technique in this book with anything other than a character's p.o.v. I don't think many writers are consciously aware of those two voices. I know until I began to hear these shifts or the lack of them from other writers in my workshops, I wasn't that aware of it either. We just shift back and forth from the character's p.o.v. to the narrator's p.o.v. and many times those shifts are very sloppy and confusing, mostly confusing in that the reader can't really tell where the information is coming from, the narrator or the character. I'm seeing that in a lot of novels now, usually not the better writers who simply 'know' what to do without conscious thought, but in most popular fiction it's fairly common. In my workshops I tell the writers that my purpose is to put them in control of their writing. I think the best writers have most control and as they write they gain more and more control over their writing.

Rhythmically yours,
Rose

Depth In Characters

[Q: How do you give characters reality without being autobiographical?]

I am a firm believer in the adage: character is story.

Characters: I seem to have to sneak up on them. Let me explain. Most often I come up with a situation that I'm interested in exploring, for example, Wallace Stegner's idea of the dilemma of the western writer, i.e., what makes the consciousness of the western writer different and almost the antithesis of the consciousness of the eastern writer.

First of all I either agree or disagree with that idea, and then I begin to ask questions about what is it that makes this true or not. In this particular case, I agree, that there is a difference between a western and eastern consciousness. I examine my own consciousness, a western one, and those of friends and acquaintances from the east. Anecdotes pop up, experiences both significant and trivial, and usually several will stick in my mind. For example the concept of space, the relationship an individual has with an environment that is overwhelmingly large and empty. I also begin to wonder what kind of people are produced by such an environment which leads me to the archetype of the cowboy.

At that point I begin to write short stories in which the focus is on various aspects of the western consciousness. I introduce a character, usually autobiographic at first, but just enough of me to breath life into the character. Then I'll write any number of stories on that particular theme, and each time the character becomes less me and more a new individual. I even write poetry on the idea, but through the consciousness of a character.

Many times in these short stories I'll change the name of the character, develop some new attitudes, etc. and will leave it that way, but eventually, after maybe a year or so, I'll go back, look at these stories as a thematic group, and find, it's all the same character, and in the last story she/he is complete, a combination of all the previous stories. And most importantly, the character is a totally new human being, not me at all. Maybe what I should be or could be or shouldn't and couldn't be, but in any case, the character is uniquely their own person, of the west and one who exemplifies certain qualities of the west that I believe are true.

You can see the setting already is there. Concepts, ideas, everything we know, takes place in a specific environment that directly effects us, so in my mind it is logical to start with an idea you want to explore, find the setting it naturally occurs in, then put a character into that setting and explore everything.

One other thing I do. I send certain of these stories out to see if I'm doing what I want. [not all of them are of publishable quality, anecdotes, scenes, etc.] When I'm really on track, they are accepted immediately. When I'm way off, there's a form reject. When I'm almost there, I get suggestions, or regrets, please send more, etc. I use these as an indication of how close I am.

Characteristically yours, Rose

Politics in Writing

Q. [Thoughts on the undercurrent of politics found in popular fiction]

I've been thinking about what makes conservative writers different than liberal/middle of the road/other writers, and what it seems to boil down to is that the conservative writers have a political agenda that determines characterization and plot. Having a political agenda is perfectly acceptable but the problem, it seems to me, is that you limit your audience to those who basically agree with you, which in a sense is nothing more than literary-political masturbation.

I've read Tom Clancy, Dale Brown, and quite a few other writers who clearly have a conservative agenda. Clancy concentrates on the plot line, with central characters who embody all the traditional values of the male: physical aggressiveness, tender protectiveness toward their weaker loved ones, always female or children, a mild, very mild regret at having to destroy their enemies, but what the hell, they asked for it by challenging the USA. Because these are traits found in most of the popular heroes in this type of novel, it strikes me as being less than serious writing. They're using a prototype character, which means there is some other message here that is more important than the human message. The plot lines are also prototypical, with the hero always winning in the end, but at some sacrifice to himself.

Brown goes further than Clancy in laying political blame on 'the liberal establishment', which means anyone that opposes war, massive armament, the pentagon, etc. etc. The central characters are cut outs, one dimensional, and they fulfill all the expectations for a reader who doesn't like to be faced with complexity and contradictions, which is also the heart of characterization. Their responses to various situations are always predictable, which may instill in the reader a feeling of glee or satisfaction, but rarely of thought. In most conservative novels of this genre, the central character borders on the superhero in his [always male] ability to resist, dominate, destroy whatever is perceived as evil. And he is totally focused with no doubts or misgivings. This character isn't created; he's cut out of a pre-existing pattern, which tells me the writer isn't interested in the humanity of the character but his political correctness.

Both Clancy and Brown have an almost sexual love of technology. Brown goes into the same kind of detail on aircraft that Sidney Sheldon goes into with sex. Clancy does the same. I find it interesting that this love of technology appears to be based on the dependability of technology, which replaces the human element, but if you think about it, the superheroes are a form of technology themselves in their similar qualities of loyalty, dependability and predictability.

I picked up a novel the other day and began to read, with no idea who the writer was. It turned out to be his first novel. In any case, the plot line was okay: CIA brings NKVD defector to US, gives him asylum knowing the defector was a serial killer. [I did wonder how this version of the CIA fit into Machiavelli's dictum of the use of spies to avoid war and/or to successfully fight a war.] The defector begins to commit very horrible mutilation killings and the reader is told within the first two pages that the reason the defector is out on the streets is that a liberal, child-molesting-judge freed him. No blame on the CIA bringing him here in the first place, nothing about that, but clearly the whole problem here stems from that liberal child molesting judge.

Most of the problems the heroes of these conservative writers seem to be caused by these liberal characters who also are unethical and immoral. That seems to me to be reducing the conflict to its most simplistic level, which doesn't allow for any searching for truth within the novel. In fact, most of the novels in this conservative genre start out with an assumption of truth and then develop the novel to demonstrate that truth. This does please the readers who are not interested in questions and it reassures them that their view of the world is the right one. For me, this puts all novels of this genre in the pure entertainment class. They explore nothing, reveal nothing, discover nothing. And in novel after novel the same idea is played out, with a change in scene, mostly depending upon who is viewed as the natural enemy that month. This is formula writing, pure and simple.

An interesting consistency in the denouement of these stories is that the triumph of the hero is usually a secret because he's working for national defense, so his heroic deeds are only understood by an elite that supports the hero-warrior. The secret heroic action, done with only the knowledge of a power elite, does send a message to the readers from the power elite, that I find very disturbing: 'Don't worry, we know what we're doing, but we can't tell you.'

There is a very definite feeling of an elite in these stories…the elite warrior, the elite support group, and the self sacrifice of the elite to defend the unwashed masses who will never understand what has been done for them. The environment these elite heroes move in is simplistic, black and white, good and evil, but the irony is that this black and white world needs to be re-defined from time to time by one of these warrior heroes.

A major message is coming through very clearly. A quote from Machiavelli demonstrates the basic philosophy of the conservative superhero: "All armed prophets succeed whereas unarmed ones fail." In his book Warrior Politics Kaplan points out the number of armed prophets who succeeded versus the unarmed ones who failed, with Jesus as the exception. Kaplan goes on to cite Machiavelli's philosophy that supports the conservative superhero image with this idea: "Values – good or bad – Machiavelli says, are useless without arms to back them up…' Thus the love of technology.

For me, the kind of writing that stresses everything over characterization, removes itself from serious consideration as good writing and becomes basically propaganda. And in my view, this kind of novel, putting out this kind of message, is truly un-American.

Democratically yours, Rose

Creating Anyone In Fiction

[Q: Can you give me a set of guidelines I could use for creating a character?]

Creating focal or central characters in fiction who are truly effective, seems to be based on pulling a core of their personality out of the writer's being, something way down deep in there (that infamous black hole?) that gives each of us individual dimension as a person. Those deep essences of our being are what make us interesting if we have them or boring if we don't. Or it makes a boring writer if s/he refuses to explore those essences.

These essences are something that, like a dark star, cause us to move, react, think in particular ways that we may be unaware of while moving through our reality. But while creating fiction, we begin to see and examine that quality through the characters, giving it to them, which adds a dimension to them that makes us want to explore who they are, given that quality.

I think that explorative nature with the character, gives a story pace, that is, because I (the writer) am in a process of discovery myself, the reader will feel that and share in that discovery. The joy of that discovery is usually in the first draft. The subsequent drafts involve the joy of shaping the language, selecting the precisely right words, the phrases that will illuminate the events in the book. The thing is, the reader only sees the finished piece, but what they feel in it, is that creative drive writers experience in creating the character and the story. This rewriting process is what moves fiction beyond therapy, which some 'writers' never get past.

I think we give those essences to our characters, and because they have that element of deep reality in them, the characters that appear around them are generated by them. That makes the writing fascinating on another level for the writer. We are discovering what that element in us means.

It seems to me when writers pull those elements of a memorable character out of ourselves, we are reducing ourselves to the essential core of being; the question is, how many times can you do that, how much of yourself can you put into your fiction? This may explain burnout.

The more complex you are as a human being, the more there is in there to explore and complexity is not a quick fix, it is not an instant mashed potatoes product. It is a result of engaging yourself totally as a human being, intellectually and physically.

And in total contradiction to what I think, here is a quote from an Annie Proulx interview on her book *Accordion Crimes*: "I have no sympathy for my characters. I'm not close to them, I don't think of them as living human beings. They are there to carry the story, they are constructs."

She says her mental plots arrive with a beginning, a middle and an end but she always starts at the end. "It's easier—one know where one's going. Writers who start without knowing exactly where they're going may find themselves in a boxed canyon."

My reaction is that Ms Proulx has revealed some of the problems with her writing and most specifically with Accordion Crimes. I shudder to think of the number of people whose reality is shaped essentially by something other than themselves. The TV Guide replaces The Koran and The Bible, Oprah and Dr. Ruth replace the teachings of Buddha and Mohammad, and Brokaw, Rather and Jennings replace the prophets. So what are we are left with? Editors who want writers to create characters with whom everyone can identify. I assume this means one or two dimensional characters. Maybe that's why Ms Proulx doesn't like her characters; they're too real.

Dark Star-ingly yours, Rose

Shifting From Linear to Cyclical Mode

[One of the inevitable questions that come in workshops for beginning writers, is 'How do you work?]

A PBS program involved a research psychologist from the University of Chicago whose book on creativity had just been released. In addition to most of the standard twaddle one hears about creativity, there was one bit that interested me: how writers make the daily transition from their linear, everyday lives to their non-linear, creative life. The author (name escapes me) studied 90 or so 'creative' people and found that each had their own way of making the transition, from sitting in the sun and staring at the horizon, to yoga, to taking a drink or two, or three, or…well that one wasn't too successful. Anyway, I wondered what some of you did to make that shift, or if you had to make that shift, or if you found it to be no problem.

As for myself, if I can start to work writing each morning before anything else is done, I have no problem. My problem comes when I find myself in a situation such as I'm in now, in which I must get up at 5:45, commute 1 hour, teach an hour and 35 minute class four days a week, commute back 1 hour, prep for the next day, and then begin my creative work. I find it's almost impossible. I'm an early morning writer. Afternoons I can edit, work on submissions, do some rewrites, but I find it impossible to create. So I just live with it for the time (six weeks). Luckily I am in a situation where I normally toil two days a week, (Tuesday and Thursday) and work (write) the other five. I got there by deciding to sacrifice things like new cars, new clothing, eating out, etc. I did not, however, give up wine.

One thing I used to do was rise at 5:30 a.m., go for a 10k run, five days a week, then come back and write. I loved that. The 10k run (about an hour of easy running) cleansed my mind and body and really put me in a creatively open state. During the run I would always focus on the day's problem in the book or story and work things out. Then I blew a knee and could no longer run. I dreamt about running. And I didn't find the bicycle a meditative instrument. So for a while I found myself outside, planting, digging, weeding, all very non linear stuff. But in the last few years, I've taken up hiking and backpacking. I try to get in a good fast 3 mile walk every day, which really cleans the system and gives me time to let my mind drift. I always walk alone, and usually I backpack alone for the same reason. Or I write posts like this for the Asilomar Topica file. Also very non linear.

Yours in meditation, Rose

The Writer As Cultural Hero

I don't think writers have ever been cultural heroes until after the fact. Those writers who were considered cultural heroes were just pop figures, the darlings of the popular critics, who always have an agenda alien to writers.

For example during the English Romantic era you had Southey more admired than the big three, Byron, Keats and Shelley, all of whom were relegated to exile by the reading public for things unrelated to writing. Later critics resurrected these non heroes to heroic stature. A modern example is Faulkner, who was totally ignored and even ridiculed when his novels first were published, and later, due to academics who admired his writing and taught it, he was resurrected by the critics. Critics rarely get it right the first time.

I think what we may be talking around is the difference between a writer who is widely known vs a writer who is a cultural hero. We live in a audio-visual age, not tied to the written word, so it seems to me that a writer can't be a 'cultural hero' but Michael Jackson can. Is Sidney Sheldon a cultural hero? Erica Jong? John Grisham? Elizabeth George? Tom Clancy? In the U.S.A. you'd have to say they qualify, but not because of their talent as writers, but through their talent to entertain with writing. They are rewarded by the culture with money, the one thing we value most and by which we all measure success.

This is a consumer culture first and last, and writers who do become ephemeral cultural heroes, are consumed but disappear once the product they produce has lost its taste. What you see then is the constant repackaging of the writer by the publisher, who also demands that the writer continue to write the same kind of fiction. The new and improved product con. In that same vein, in the past few years we've seen a new packaging tool, the recognized author writing with a co-author. I'm not sure what that is. Perhaps introducing a new product with the blessing of the old product. There is a lot of junk food writing going on. By definition, a cultural hero is a product of the culture and America produces cultural heroes that reflect its image. Writers rarely do that. Makes you wonder about Elvis, though, doesn't it?

A writer of serious fiction occasionally may get some recognition, usually due to winning one of the better known literary prizes, but for the most part, after the initial rush to read, so they'll have something intellectual to talk about at the next party, the reading public drops them too. Consumers don't savor. They consume. They don't re-read, and generally they don't read in depth because intellectually, they bring too little to serious writing to understand depth. The *N.Y. Times Best Seller List* is in actuality a literary version of a MacDonald's menu. Once in a while you may find something nourishing there, but the general menu is fast food, meant to be consumed quickly and forgotten. And now we have the t.v. version of the *NY Times Best Seller List*, the Oprah Selections. Sigh.

I have this image in my mind of modern, 'literate' Americans: they drive a new vehicle that costs more than a majority of the people in the world will earn in a lifetime, listening to books on tape with a cellular phone growing out of one ear. They are like water bugs, skimming along the surface of life. For an 'in depth' conversation about writing they read reviews in *The NY Review of Books* or *Time* or *Newsweek*, or, if they're really intellectual, *Atlantic, Harpers* and *The Smithsonian,* and they listen to T*erry Gross Fresh Air show* on PBS.

Literary cultural heroes may exist in other countries primarily due to a long tradition of literature or a non existent tradition of consumerism. Poets and novelists in Russia, South America, and Japan come to mind. When America can fill a football stadium to capacity to hear a poet read her/his works, then I'd say we have a literary cultural hero on our hands. I am not anticipating a shortage of tickets.

So, Vonnegut's departure from the scene because writers aren't cultural heroes any more, indicates a very limited knowledge of cultural heroes, unless he's referring to the pre literate age when the teller of tales was a major figure in the community. I don't think he is.

Now honestly, group, does anyone here really entertain the idea of becoming a cultural hero? Aside from me I mean.

Humbly yours, Rose

Establishing Rhythms II

Okay, here is another technique I use and it seems to work well, especially in very intense passages where I want not just the language (words), but the syntax (structure) to intensify the moment.

I write my prose passage as it comes to me in the flow of the piece (novel or short story), and then I go back and polish it a bit, making certain I have the power words I want in there, not too many, not too few. I also am very aware of which voice I'm using, third or first, distant or close, because the rhythms of each is very different. Some passages work well in distant, but for me, the most powerful passages are in close voice, and those are the ones that require very careful shaping, because this is the character's voice.

Once I've done determined the voice I want, I have to go back and change the way the syntax works because I have to think about the impact I want this passage to have on the reader. With a distant voice, I'm striving for clarity. With a close voice I'm striving for emotional content. Once I begin changing the syntax of individual lines, I am forced to reselect words that work with the rhythm and the voice. This goes on for a while and eventually I reach a point where I think the piece is ready, I read it into a tape recorder, exactly as I've written it with no dramatic voice shifts that aren't already there on the page and straight through to the end. Then I listen to that as I edit the written words to get the rhythms right. Then I put it back into the usual prose format of a paragraph. You'd be amazed at the power it has. With the close voice, the more you know about your character the more natural the flow of his voice will be.

Oh, by the way, I wrote a series of short stories over quite a long time with continuing characters, settings, etc, and eventually it turned into a collection that looked an awful lot like a novel. Each story was a unit, complete, but as the reader progresses through the collection, they realize that information given in previous stories is referred to by the characters,and not necessarily reestablished each time. The characters relate to each other based on previous experiences, and in fact some experiences lead into the next one. I didn't intend to do that when I began, but I got so fascinated by these characters I couldn't stop writing about them. But the one thing that tied them all, was the first person narrator, Hoover, who had a very particular style of thought and speech, and a totally unique view of his world, and that's what made the various stories work well. It was his speech patterns I had to discover.

Unfortunately my fascination for the collection isn't reflected by publishers; about 15 of the stories have been published individually but the collection crouches here in the womb of my computer awaiting birth. So far, not even one damned labor pain. The collection is called The Holy City Zoo, in honor of an abandoned religious cult town in California, near which I lived at one time. Some of the characters are based, very loosely, on some of the people I knew then. I had to clean a couple of them up. Oh, I could tell you stories, and probably will.

as usual, Rose aka Pussytoes

Evil As A Literary Theme

I too am very interested in the nature of evil in people we think are like us, and who in fact probably are in every way except for that hollowness of soul which has been replaced by a ready made identity, which can range from the rabid Dallas Cowboy fan to the corporate executives of R.J. Reynolds Tobacco Corporation who can state with apparent total conviction that cigarette smoking doesn't harm your health.

The horror of this is that these people really believe in what they are saying or doing. They have to, else their lives mean nothing. Deep down inside, when they peel away the layers of identity they've taken on, there is nothing, a terrible vacuum, and if they ever face that they have two choices: death or denial. This is the existential moment of absurdity, when the setting of one's life falls apart and you are left with what you are.

For too many modern Americans, this means they are left with nada. And Hemingway said it for us,

"Our nada who art in nada, nada be thy name thy kingdom nada, they will be nada…"

Buckminster Fuller stated, "aggression is a secondary behavior of humans-…when they get what they need, when they need it, and are not overwhelmed, they are spontaneously benevolent; it is only when they become desperate that they become aggressive because what they have relied on is no longer working."

We seem to have become a desperate country, overwhelmed by problems.

This kind of benevolence is an echo of Neitzsche's Superman, in which the powerful give just enough to the weak to keep them dependent but not enough to give them the strength to challenge them.

All of which leads me to taking on evil as a writer of fiction. It seems to me that fiction writers take on evil in various ways, depending upon the nature of evil they are concerned with. If you take on an absolute evil you almost force yourself into the area of an intellectual understanding of evil, a discussion and examination of it, for example an allegory. This has a limited audience but because that audience is more of a 'reader elite,' having an effect on that evil may be more likely due to the audience being the intellectual movers and shakers of a culture. This doesn't happen much any more in fiction. For example, the movers and shakers are reading non fiction philosophy, such as *Warrior Politics*, and using that as a basis for forming our foreign policy.

Then we have the possibility of examining specific evils in the various genres such as science fiction, speculative, literary, mystery, etc. I suppose any genre can lend itself to an examination of evil, and the level of evil determines the approach, i.e., the more 'entertaining' the work the less intense is the examination of evil. For example, a mystery is dealing with the evil of murder, but it's not the evil nature of killing that drives the book, it's bringing the evil doer to justice, and even that is downplayed in most mysteries. The killer is only interesting because her/his act of murder, brings out the hunter-detective, who is also not really interested in evil. It's just a job, ma'am. We become more interested in the character who is pursing the evil, than the evil itself. And once the murderer is brought to justice, "God is in his heaven, all is right with the world."

A good example of a writer who makes the examination of evil, 'fun' or 'entertaining,' is Dickens. He clearly has a social agenda, and his character's names and personalities approach allegory, but it was the 'rollicking good tale' that was of more interest in most of his novels. I think that's still what we have today, but television has replaced Dickens to a great degree, so for the fiction writer there has to be a different approach.

TV and movies have a casual approach to evil, that is, their attitude seems to be, yeah, this is evil and watch us kill it. They set up arch villains, really nasty, baby killing types so the revenge of the 'heroes' will be greatly anticipated and justified. This gave rise to the anti hero, the character who was as bad as all the bad guys, but he was our bad guy. Clint Eastwood in spaghetti westerns or as Dirty Harry comes to mind.

I think there is an element of evil in almost everything we write. Evil seems to be the base element of conflict, and the degree to which we emphasize it, determines the way the work will be received, possibly even the genre we select.

When was the last time you read a work of fiction that was so passionate about the subject, that it changed the way you perceived the particular evil being dealt with? I think that is the aim of most serious writers of fiction. The difference between the various genres may be the focus on evil, how it is emphasized or de-emphasized.

I think what it boils down to for me is this; we choose the genres we write in depending upon the passion we feel about evil and the necessity to examine it.

Passionately yours, Rose

Re: Female Character

I'm not certain this will help but my approach to creating male or female characters has more to do with who they are in a given situation. I know they are who they are partly due to gender, but overall I try to go for the human aspect of the character. When you're dealing with stereotypes, clichés, etc. naturally you make the characters predictably one gender or another, and they react predictably, but that's not really writing and they're not really characters.

I shoot for that fourth dimension of characterization, the unique world view, self view, the coming to awareness of what else they are as they face whatever conflicts they may face. I love reading about the opposite gender and seeing them do the exact right thing for who they are, not what they are. And by exact right thing, I don't mean in the sense of right or wrong as a moral or ethical judgment, but the exact right thing for who they are. I always have the reaction of, Yes! That is exactly what he/she would do!

Example: I have a female character who 'collects' the flaws and weaknesses of her husband and rebuilds him in that image so she can gain the mental strength to begin to live her own life. But, as she reaches the perfectly flawed image of what he is, she goes beyond flaws and begins to look for fear, which she also finds, which changes her goal from being purely individual to something larger than herself. She comes to understand something about life in general rather than just her life.

One of the places she looks for weaknesses is during and after sex. And she collects various kinds of weaknesses, physical and emotional. These she called (and I have to say it was her idea, not mine…it was one of those moments when the phrase popped out so quickly I didn't really have time to think about where it came from) "the fucking truth." With the emphasis on the second word. Anyway, my point here is that at this point in the novel, she became a true individual and from that point on her world view became uniquely hers. I was searching for her character even as she was, and we both discovered it at the same time.

Well, I do hope I've managed to confuse the issue as much as possible.

As usual, smelling as sweet by any other name, Rose

Literary Baggage

Q: "Isn't it time we finally got past Hemingway?

For some reason that comment set me off in various directions, like the 13 Ways of Looking At A Blackbird (which I also can't get past) and arriving at the point Stevens made, "I do not know which to prefer,/ The beauty of inflections/Or the beauty of innuendoes,/The blackbird whistling/Or just after."

I'm not sure what Amy meant exactly. Perhaps it was, can't we get past the male image that Hemingway was examining, or maybe, can't we just get past Hemingway altogether.

I knew it was dangerous mentioning Hemingway; he has fallen into so much disfavor by academics, critics, writers etc., but I am still fascinated by what he did with the language. I can't get past that. And I don't think I ever will.

I began to examine that reaction, i.e., why don't or can't I move on? I think is has to do with my 'hoarding' nature, that is, I don't consume, I gather, collect, examine, and treasure these pricelessly crafted images of man's nature, realizing that as I write I'm building on what they established. A good part of what Hemingway created, can't be consumed like Clancy or Robbins, who are truly are consumed. And those suckers come back on you, hon.

In any case, my literary baggage is, I admit, excessive, and ever growing, but I can't bear to part with any of them. I'll never get them in the baggage compartment above my head or under the seat. I'll have to charter my own cargo plane. Or fleet of them.

I am selective, but I'll never get past them. That's like asking, "Can't you get past the fact that you were born?" No, I can't. "Can't you get past your childhood?" No, it's still a part of me, as is every other phase of my life. I am the sum total of my experience, and Cather, Hemingway, Stevens, Joyce, Eliot, Chaucer, Mailer, Dickinson, Austen, etc. etc. are part of that experience.

This doesn't mean that I'm not still reading new [to me] writers, I am, and I'm adding them to my horde, writers like Ivan Doig, Charles Frazier, Sebastian Faulk, and others I'm still reading and trying to understand. Some I can get past. Others I can't, for the same reason Hemingway stays with me.

A theme I find myself addressing over and over is the idea of consumption as the disease of the 20th century. I think the best seller lists are a good example of consumption in writing, not just by readers, but by writers, editors, publishers and critics as well. The shelf life of a book today demonstrates the intensity of consumption to the exclusion of all else, as do book auctions, promotion trips, t.v. ads, etc. etc. I anticipate a label on books that says, 'Best consumed by 2/23/04.'

If we begin to see our own creations as products to be sold and consumed, then we can get past them. If we see them as something else, we can't. And shouldn't.

A bit of personal data: my study, the entire house, looks like several museums exploded and the random fall out filled the place. Over my pc is a poster from the workers strike in Poland in 1980; on the wall above that, a leopard skin, a pair of snow shoes, a hand painted board with the Emerson quote on a foolish consistency, a Mexican mask, a painting done by an Oakland street jazz musician, a full length dancing mask and cape from the Gold Coast, and on various wine boxes cum bookcases sit a top hat, a candle stick with a metal rainbow trout, an Indian drum, a photo of a folk singer in Moscow taken by a friend of mine, a pot from Costa Rica, a chollo cactus lamp, an ancient Corona portable typewriter, a pot metal statue of a WW I doughboy, a laughing, rubber Buddha, a piece of the Berlin Wall, and all this seen without moving my head. I don't even dare look behind me. The books loom in ever higher bookcases and stacks. I come by my hoarding nature, naturally.

Which leads me to the next idea:

Moral Stance of The Writer or Writer As Character

I wonder about novelists taking a moral stand in their work. When I read one of the classics, I have a feeling that when writers are most effective they are reflecting a moral stance of the culture through the characters, or perhaps examining a moral stance. The instant they *begin* to inject their own moral stance [that is in the distant voice, not the close] the book loses its power to move and becomes an interesting autobiographical footnote, usually to the detriment of the novel itself. I find myself becoming impatient with personal philosophies either interrupting the narrative flow, or characters becoming mouthpieces for the author's own beliefs. Ayn Rand springs to mind. (and immediately springs out again)

The idea of a writer becoming her/his character or drawing upon their own anguish, etc to give the characters a passionate base, interests me because it is a very tricky approach to writing. It is so close to autobiography it can lose its way and simply become that, which is less than fiction, which, as I'm sure you're all tired of hearing me say, is intensified reality. I think we all draw from ourselves to a degree, but to draw too much seems to me to be moving toward confessional therapy. At some point the character has to come to life outside the writer and when that happens, true fiction happens.

A classic example of that type of self examination is Hemingway, who might more accurately be described as one of the greatest and most sensitive American male psychotics, who spent his entire writing life examining what it meant to be male or how one became a man, but never finding an answer, which was his answer. (don't you love layered sentences?) Hemingway was his characters.

I think at his best, he was truly examining the condition of the western male, and at his worst, he was giving us his philosophy of life. The two coexist in almost every novel and short story, but I think the examination of the western male dominated, which was what made him a great writer. His examination was so unique, so intense, it could not be denied.

I feel great pain coming from him in his novels and the spare style he employs is, to me, the inarticulate but passionate male, squeezing words out in an attempt to express the joy and pain of a male's life. (I'm using male to be clear that it's not just Hemingway's life) I think Hemingway's style is also an example of form and content and meaning, being beautifully fused.

Just as Hemingway never can quite find the ritual or the male guide to lead him on into masculinity, he also can never quite express his pain or joy in other than brief, staccato bursts, or in spare but lyric descriptions of nature, war and death, subjects males are, or were, allowed to by lyric about. Women, love and sex are subjects he remains inarticulate about. Many of the classic movie heroes are based on this inarticulate male, John Wayne, Jimmy Stewart, Randolph Scott, Clint Eastwood etc. which most males find accurate or at least empathetic. Hemingway carried the inarticulate male to artistic heights.

If you want to understand the white American middle class male who still dominates this culture, you need to read Hemingway. And in the reading of his works you will understand why his life ended as it did. I think that is one of the dangers of becoming your own character.

I would like to add one thing. I think I would hate Hemingway as a person. And I don't think I'd be too crazy about Tolstoy either. Or any of the Brontes. The point here is, I love them as writers, not people, and I'd be unable to feel that way, if they had dominated their books autobiographically.

as usual,

Rose (thou art sick)

Good Vs. Other Writing

I use the four divisions or categories of writers.

Division 1: the art of fiction in its finest form: Cormac McCarthy, Sebastain Faulk, Ivan Doig, etc. By the way, I'm excluding the classic writers from the past, here. Some of these writers do it book after book and some are hit and miss. I think, for me, Proulx is hit and miss; she hit it with *The Shipping News*, missed with *Accordion Crimes*, but there were writerly things in that book that kept it in Division 1 for me. McCarthy seems to have hit every time for me in his last 4 books, starting with Suttree. I loved Doig's *Montana* trilogy because it made me feel I was in the hands of a master story teller who successfully suspended my reality for his.

Division 2: genre writing in its finest form: Elmore Leonard, Dennis LeHane, James Lee Burke, John Lescroart.

Division 3: heavy on plot line, technological/factual research: Tom Clancy, Dale Brown.

Division 4: I don't read division four books [intentionally] but I know when I've inadvertently picked one up; I have the overwhelming urge to edit it. I think Harlequin Romances fall into this category. Quite aside from that, for me, when I read a writer who makes me want to write, I know I'm reading a Division 1 book. In Division 1, I keep stopping and rereading to see how they did certain things and how they keep drawing me in. I am taken by the beautiful use of language.

When I am entertained but the writer has become repetitious with success and doesn't really try to take his style to the next level, I know I'm reading bestseller list fiction. Here you see the same character, the same setting with slight variations on the plot line. These books are usually good for three, maybe four readings, then most of them become tiresome. It's a strange case of "imitation being the sincerest form of flattery," because they're imitating themselves. John Lescroart is an exception to this. His novels with two repeating characters, Abe Glitsky and Dismas Hardy, and it's always the San Francisco setting, but they seem fresh to me every time. When I read Lescroart, I am immediately lost in the story, which is what every writer wants a reader to feel. James Lee Burke is an example of a writer who is very good for three novels and then becomes a little too repetitive. He also makes glaring and major errors in point of view and tries to cover them but rather clumsily. At this bestseller level I find a lot of small mistakes in p.o.v. or phrasing, etc. Some of this line editing is due to the publisher not having competent editors, and when these errors become numerous and intrusive, it drops to Division 3.

Division 3 is totally plot, a fast read, more like junk food than anything else, it's fun to read but you don't want to read much of it. They make great slam-bang movies, i.e., lots of action, movement, not much depth. I've heard them defended by people who say the characters involved in these actions are not very deep people in reality. So? I don't like shallow people in reality, why should I in fiction?

All this said, one thing remains; good writing makes me aware that the language is being used with unusual competence. It makes me proud to be trying to do that as well. It puts me in mind of a quote by T.E. Hulme, the British poet and critic speaking about the preciseness of language in his essay 'Romanticism and Classicism:' "There are two things to distinguish, first the particular faculty of mind to see things as they really are, and apart from the conventional ways in which you have been trained to see them. This is itself rare enough in all consciousness. Second, the concentrated state of mind, the grip over oneself which is necessary in the actual expression of what one sees. To prevent one falling into the conventional curves of ingrained technique, to hold on through infinite detail and trouble to the exact curve you want. Where ever you get this sincerity, you get the fundamental quality of good art without dragging in infinite or serious."

Novels Vs. Short Stories

I can't imagine a single technique that the novelist uses that the short story writer doesn't. By technique I mean dialogue, setting, characterization, etc, etc. The major difference as I see it, is focus and within that, how complex the basic conflict of the story is.

The short story is highly focused, very intense, whereas the novel has a broader scope and probably several different focus points. This is all obvious, I would think.

The great thing about a short story as a learning process is that you can see the various techniques very highly focused and if they don't work it is clear they don't. It is less obvious in a novel. A beginning writer can go on for a hundred pages and never use dialogue, or shift out of a narrative point of view, because the pace is different, not as tight. In a short story if you do that, it collapses on you immediately. A beginning writer can fool themselves for a hell of a long time if they don't know the basic techniques and I can't think of a better place to learn them than in carefully crafted short stories.

One major thing I think new writers learn in the short story is pace and narrative pull. Without those two elements a short story will show a reader immediately that the writer has no idea of where she/he is going with the story and is hoping like hell they'll stumble across the point as they 'follow along.'

If you take the basic four point plot formula, conflict, complication, crisis, conclusion, and apply it to both the novel and the short story, you will find that the only thing that expands in the novel is the complexity of the conflict and the number of complications that come out of that. What new novelists may fail to see because of their broad scope is that the complications too easily turn into artificial hurdles that the heroine/hero must get past to get to the crisis point, instead of each complication revealing a new aspect of the character or of the conflict, always moving the story ahead. This rarely happens in a short story form because you write within actual wordage limits, which means everything has to work in harmony.

In my workshops I always stress to new writers to over write the maximum wordage of the story and then edit back, which always tightens the story line. Adding always makes it bog down.

And yes, I do give writers who work with me wordage limits to teach them how to edit. For example, if I set a 3500 word maximum and a 2500 minimum on a short story, I encourage them to write about 4000 + on the first draft. The minimum length lets them know if they have a short story or just an anecdote, an idea.

I think that many people who do go immediately to writing novels are avid readers of novels and have an almost unconscious awareness of what a novel should do or could do. They have gone through a learning process as a reader with a writer's eye and if they are lucky, that comes through for them in their writing. I also think that is very, very rare.

I vividly remember various graduate seminars in which I was always at odds with everyone else about the novels, short stories and poems being dealt with. I finally understood it was the approach; I was reading as a writer; they were reading as critics.

But, I think everyone could learn a hell of a lot more about their own writing by writing short stories. And they could discover new things as well. The whole idea here is to gain control of your writing, isn't it?

Racial Identity of Characters

[Q: Don't readers have the innate ability to identify race in a character by voice alone?]

I do believe that you're right to a degree about the ability we have to identify someone's race by voice only and that ability we all have speaks to the incredible facility of our brains to process complex information very rapidly. We not only take into consideration what is said, the diction, vocabulary, grammar, but also the syntax, the rhythms, the stresses. I think the degree of accuracy each individual has depends upon the degree of language facility, conscious or unconscious. I know people who are barely literate, or functionally illiterate who have an incredible, unconscious language facility. This may be an innate talent of human beings, i.e., we sort out who is whom in order to protect ourselves. But there are also people who are functionally literate who have no language sensitivity at all. Like critics and agents. No, no, sorry, just a joke.

However, we have a growing number of people of various races who speak 'the king's English,' and cannot be identified by voice only. Othello immediately comes to mind. The question with Othello, is, is his race of critical importance, or is it his gender? On a more contemporary note, close your eyes and listen to Carl Lewis, the Olympic long jumper. Standard, non-identifiable English. It's much like the mid-Atlantic accent newscasters strive for, no regional identity at all . I understand the Olympic bomber spoke very few words: "There is a bomb in the Olympic park. You have thirty minutes." When you just read it, it has no identity. It would be an interesting exercise to rewrite the lines and give them identity, and to see which lines each of us believes to be what racial derivation and why. It also can be a process of eliminating possible identities.

Stereotypes immediately jump out, and I have to admit that we all deal in stereotypes, so are they accurate? As you said, yes, most of the time. So, is it racist to say what the FBI and police said, i.e., the bomber is not black? Yes and no. If it's accurate, a judgment made based upon experience, then no, it's not racist. If it's only a result of prejudice and prejudgment, then it's not accurate and is in fact racism. This case involves an ironic twist: they didn't hear certain aural clues, accent, tone, etc, so they assumed the caller was white. The implication is that certain non white groups have an instantly recognizable voice.

Would it have been racist if the caller's words were stereotypical in some way, the syntax, grammar, use of scatological language, and he was identified by the police as a minority? Example: "There be a bomb in the f……ing Olympic park. You got thirty motherf…ing minutes."

What was your immediate reaction to that? If you were uneasy or nervous that I would phrase it that way, that means you too reacted to the language with a particular racial identification. There are only two words in that version that might identify it as of a particular race; one is grammatical, one is scatological. Is that racist? It clearly is a stereotype, but how accurate is it? Do any other groups use that particular grammatical construct? If not, then it's accurate and it is not racial. The problem here is that if you presented those lines to a group of people, most would be reluctant to identify it for fear of being called a racist, but that in itself says the identification is fairly accurate.

When you get out of slang, scatology and grammar, and there is no accent, you're left with tones, rhythms, the music of the language. Okay, how does an Arab sound? An Ethiopian? A Pakistani? An Indian (from India)? Can you identify an American Indian using English, say a Navajo or a Hopi? Is their language use different than Sioux or Utes?

If the words of the bomber had been written instead of spoken, could you identify the gender? Age? Race? Exercise: write a two person dialogue in which what they say reveals what they are. Keep business and tags to a minimum.

One final point: as you read through this collection of rhetorical questions, you are assuming certain things about me, my gender, my race, my ethnic background, etc., but none of the people on this board, not one, knows me personally. What causes people to make these assumptions about who I am, what I am? The language, pure and simple. The way my words march, prance, stumble, blunder, flit and fly, gives people an image of who I am, but if one examines that image, it is purely abstract. This is why I love dialogue.

Anonymously yours, Rose (is that my first or last name? is it a nickname? how does that name relate to the name in my e-mail address?)

Politics And The Writer

I agree that if one is writing with more than entertainment in mind, and sometimes even with that, you are connected with politics. Writers are creatures of their environment, and as writers a significant part of our environment is the acquisition of information, sometimes random and accidental but more often deliberate. Writers absorb information accidentally reading newspapers, watching t.v. and movies, etcetera, but there is the difference between a writer and a non writer; writers absorb that information, it becomes part of their intellectual being. Non writers pass most of it through their intellectual system without processing it, thus it has no intellectual nutritional value. Kind of a MacDonald's of the mind, a.k.a. the evening news on CBS,NBC,ABC, CNN, etc.

Choice of subject, setting, everything in fiction has political ramifications, even down to the point of view one chooses. The difference from writer to writer is how they choose to emphasize or play down those political ramifications. And controlling all that, is each individual writer's consciousness, the sum total of her/his being. Writers who are aware of this political aspect of fiction manipulate it, use it, refine it or play it down as much as possible. Writers who remain unconscious of it, still use it but it's not as effective and sometimes it can compromise the work.

Problems In Writing Science Fiction

I think one of the ideas in creating science fiction that interests me as a writer is the need to create a new, logically unified reality. The problem is that once you create this alternative reality in your story, most of it has to be imitative of the reality we know. The readers must suspend their disbelief in many areas for science fiction to work, and for me, the more a writer depends upon that 'willing suspension of disbelief' the weaker the work is as fiction. This is the 'yeah but' syndrome, in which each collapse of this reality the writer is trying to establish is met with the "Yeah, but..." and then the excuse that it's science fiction so it's acceptable.

Making up unpronounceable names from consonants, numbers, symbols, etc, are part of the shallow reality being created. I've also found the more a science fiction story is dependent upon some sort of reality-based scientific or technological advance and jargon, the weaker the overall writing is. What too much science fiction writing does is tell a very standard story with cliché science fiction characters and settings. They depend upon the limitations of the genre for their success as a story teller, not the story.

I think one of the most limiting things about science fiction is the fact that it is almost impossible to create a new reality, a new world, populated by a new kind of life form with it's own form of communication. Even my description of the problem is limited because we can only communicate with our language references. A totally new reality with its own logic simply can't be done, so the science fiction writer is limited to a basic conflict situation; human beings explore new worlds and come into contact with new realities and they can only communicate their understanding of it in normal human terms. It's the old Columbus-DeSoto-Magellan story, i.e., how do you react to a world you've never seen, populated by people you had no idea existed, and alive with plant and animal life beyond your experience? You react to it in terms you are familiar with and deal with it with reactions that have worked before.

This also means the science fiction writers depend upon a science fiction mind set in their readers, a sort of subconscious shorthand in which phrases like <time warp> or <traveling at cee> both innovative ideas, can imply an entire technological reality that some other writer has established before. The more a writer depends upon this science fiction mind set, the weaker the writing is. They don't bother to establish the logical reality for each story and depend upon previous established realities. The best overall example I can give of this is the *Star Trek/Star Wars* genre, in which not only the realities of various universes have been established but the characters as well. What you get is imitation on imitation on imitation. The genre simply gets more complicated, not more complex. It expands horizontally, not vertically; that is it doesn't push the genre into new areas, (vertical expansion) it simply plays with the already established areas, (horizontal expansion). That seems to me to be the problem with most popular science fiction.

There are new writers out there, however, who are pushing the vertical expansion of science fiction, moving into areas that are very new, very interesting. Sheila Finch for example is exploring the idea of an elite group of beings called "lingsters," whose talent for communication is the most valued in the cosmos. She's worked out a very original reality there based on the concept that the one thing any exploration needs is communication. The focus here is examining a logical problem human beings would have with any kind of exploration of space and contacting new life forms and the kind of society that would logically grow out of that. What she's doing is taking the idea of Why Johnny Can't Read, the resulting growth of a literate elite, and making that the focus of space exploration. Another thing she does is write character based novels, rather than idea based or gimmick based [tech science fiction].

The problem with creating alternative reality characters is that they would be so alien, there would be no way to create them other than in relation to human beings, so they become simply reflections of distortions of human reality, not a reality unto themselves. Think about science fiction aliens; most of them are anthropomorphic in various ways, from physical appearances to emotional-intellectual drives. This is clearly because readers need something with which to identify and it's a problem no other genre has, and which probably limits traditional science fiction writing. Non traditional science fiction writing has the possibility of going in another direction, that is taking a single human quality and making it the essence of a new being, which is essentially is allegoric.

In genres outside science fiction, the exploration has to do with human beings, who seem to be infinitely complex and constantly expanding, changing, even as their environment changes at a pace outside their control. The point is that I believe humanity is as complex as the universe, and so the possibilities of exploration are greater. The one thing that makes human beings more complex is that what makes them most interesting is the immeasurable, the unquantifiable; the spirit, the soul, our mentality. Good science fiction writers take that complexity and project it out into space.

Hard core science fiction writers are tied to the reality of various levels physics, and either taking them out to a logical end, or postulating a world in which certain physical laws don't apply. What makes their writing interesting is limited to playing with physics, like the idea of E=MC2 as the basis for the speed at which exploratory vehicles travel, that is at "cee", and then the endless argument about reaching maximum velocity instantly in outer space, so if you fire a missile at some target, does the missile reach maximum velocity instantly and travel in company with the vehicle firing it, or not? How far can you take that in a novel without turning it into a fictional physics text? I heard a comedian once ask this question: "If you're in a vehicle traveling at the speed of light, and you turn your headlights on, does anything happen? "

A very common theme in science fiction is to take human beings who are exactly like us and put them in a futuristic, technological situation and introduce an alien, who usually turns out to be a monster whose one purpose is to eat, absorb, digest, and otherwise destroy human beings. The Frankenstein-Wolfman-Dracula story, and the new monsters still have those human qualities of the old monsters. Example, in *Alien*, it's a mother monster, called a 'bitch' by Sigourny Weaver's character. The horror of that monster and most monsters, is that it embodies some basic human nightmares, i.e., *monsters erupting* out of monsters' mouths, or growing inside human beings (an interesting idea here; are these male science fiction authors who are writing about the horrors of pregnancy?) and erupting through something other than an orifice that could handle it. Like your nose. We have to anthropomorphize these aliens because we have no reality to base them on, and so what we have with aliens then is a reflection of our own values, fears, etc.

It is interesting to see how science fiction writers portray these aliens because that reflects their attitude about the universe as threatening or benevolent, and their attitude about human beings and technology. The best writing I've seen in this genre is usually based more on sociological/psychological speculation, rather than on technological possibilities or improbabilities. And the best writing of this type seems to be cautionary tales.

One final word. I think the science fiction writers who are most insular, most hostile to other genres of fiction, are also the most limited. They are the ones who write in science fiction clichés, repeating concepts already established, infinitely expanding their genre horizontally, so that what we get is *Alien, Alien II, Alien III, Alien IV,* well, you get the idea. They are the ones who argue over the technological trivia. The best science fiction writers are expanding the genre vertically, making it more complex, and whose focus is what we all focus on, humanity.

Or maybe not,
Rose

Who Is A Serious Writer

[This question came up on our Art and Integrity in Fiction board, with one person stating that you can't be called a writer unless you make money from writing.]

Well, let's take this definition of a serious writer and test it a bit. Is a writer who is published in what can be called major literary magazines, where the pay is nominal, ranging from copies or $5.00 up to $100, not as serious as the writer who writes for Redbook or Cosmo and gets anywhere from $500 to $3500 dollars? Is the amount of money received the determination of the seriousness of the writer? In this definition it seems to be, thus The Bridges of Madison County is our modern War and Peace, right? How serious was the writer? Was his primary concern being published? Do serious writers sit down and say to themselves, "Well, I wonder how much money I can make today?" And where would you put Emily Dickinson or Herman Melville?

It seems to me that serious writers range from those who publish exclusively in literary magazines to those who publish in *Harpers* or *Atlantic* or *Redbook, The New Yorker,* etc. The larger markets for serious fiction are limited and very tough to break into, so in the meantime, a serious writer, whom I think writes to be read, goes where the markets are and continues to assault those markets that pay, not because of the pay, but because of the larger number of readers available there. Of course, there's always the question of how serious the readers are. For example, *Playboy* pays around $3500 for a short story, but who buys the magazine for the stories? Yeah, yeah, I know. In the 1970s I met the fiction editor at that time for Playboy and he was not very impressive as a literary judge.

I judge serious writers by what they write and how they write it. Serious writers go beyond the surface, where most entertainment writers remain. It's the difference between a mud puddle a hundred yards wide and a half inch deep, and a bottomless lake.

Serious writers write what they have to write or want to write and once it's done, they look for a market, which means looking for readers. It's nice to be rewarded handsomely in a culture that rates success by the dollar sign, but if you subscribe to the theory that you are as good as your paycheck, you made a wrong turn when you came *down that less traveled road to fiction.*

One thing I think all writers suffer from is the secret shame at not being published by a 'major publisher.' This is something we have to get over, and realize that the 'major publishers' are basically marketers looking for a product. If you don't write product material, you're probably not going to get published. Consider the 'shelf life' of a normal book: three weeks maximum. And then it's spoiled???

All of which leads to a second question: Why Write?

I honest to god don't know a simple answer to that. Yes, I like it when people read my stories and are moved by them. I like it when some anonymous editor out there selects my story to publish on the merit of the story itself and nothing else, like the comment by an editor who read one of my stories, accepted it for publication and wrote me a letter telling me my story, "made him gleeful."

I like it when I'm writing and make myself laugh or when I feel the pain of what I'm writing about. I like working with my imagination, translating an abstract idea to a concrete reality. I like shaping words into a reality that never existed before I created it. I like intensifying the life I experience around me so that readers say, "Yes! That's the way it was!"

And, confession time, I like teaching new writers what I know and seeing them full of the same joy of writing that I have when they discover they can do it and their stories begin to take on a new depth they didn't think they had. I like it when I see these new writers move on, independent of my teaching, and take the art of writing one more step forward.

I like talking to writers about our art, which is the one thing the internet does that I think is invaluable, despite the pomposity, posing and pronouncing that seems to go on occasionally.

And, finally, I like to think that what writers do is what human beings were meant to do; create.

Writers searching for compatible souls
Or
Walking through a minefield wearing
Oversized clown shoes

Like workshops and writer's conferences, the virtual world, the internet and the various writer's boards on commercial cyber hookups like AOL, Prodigy, etc., have to be very carefully approached. They are minefields, booby trapped paths through an incredibly lush jungle of ideas where lurking flamers wait for the unwary.

But, also hidden in those cyber-jungles are clearings populated by some very astute, very caring writers who are not just 'reaching out and touching someone,' they are exchanging ideas on writing, discussing the craft and their approach to it. And it is there the freelance writer can find the international network of writers that is beginning to form. In the past few years I've made at least a dozen new writer friends whom I only know as a presence in cyberspace. And there's something very interesting about that.

We know each other only through what we write, the ideas we express and how we express them. We're also beginning to discover how we create personalities through those ideas, and the great thing about this is that we are what we say, write, think, not what we look like. There are no physical traits here, unless you choose to reveal that, and there is no gender, no age, nothing but your intellect, your words. What we seem to be doing here is discovering our pure writer's personality. Everything else is secondary. And this could only happen in cyberspace.

The same applies to the real world. You can get seriously hurt in a writer's group or at a writer's conference that has no real direction but a lot of touch-feely attitudes. I wrote an article about this specific subject for an anthology, *A Writer's Guide to Southern California,* while I was a fiction workshop leader for the Santa Barbara Writer's Conference, that still, with some updates, holds true. Here it is:

The motivations for attending a writer's conference are as varied as the people who decide to attend one of these strange gatherings. And they are strange. Think of it; a group of people who spend a good portion of their time alone, in their minds, putting words on paper that they hope will be read by an audience they will never know, decide to break out of that isolation and meet with other people who are dong the same thing. Why?

I suppose basically all people attending a writer's conference are doing so to "make connections," specifically with agents, editors and publishers. This rarely happens as one expects it to; that is, you do meet some of these "connections," but that may be about all that happens.

A second reason would be to have your writing read or heard, and that does happen in most conferences, but after the conference you're still at home alone with your writing and whatever praise or criticism you received fades quickly. The only thing that has changed is that someone else might be aware you, and more significantly, you put yourself on the line as a writer. That in itself is a major step.

A third reason is to meet other writers, and this is probably the one thing you can really count on in any conference. In fact, this is the one consistency in all conferences that is truly worthwhile and lasting. If anything else positive does happen it's gravy. With that protective, cynical outlook, you might be ready to handle a writer's conference.

Each conference is unique, but there are some aspects you can look for to prepare yourself on what to expect. The most visible type of conference is essentially social. It offers lectures by the current best selling authors who are on the book tour, and usually has at least one "literary figure" appearing in some capacity. The flyers and ads for such a conference will hint, rather broadly, that there is a chance for you to meet these names as well as people in the business such as editors, agents and publishers.

This type of conference is usually held in a resort area with recreational facilities such as bars, tennis courts [both essentials], beaches, golf courses, restaurants, shopping, etc. These attractions are the clues you should take as a warning; some of the names may be there to have fun, not talk shop. Talking shop is the payment they make for the vacation, and they try to keep this payment as low as possible. And sad to say, most of the names don't really believe anything productive comes out of a writer's conference.

This is not to say that a social conference will not offer workshops, but you have to realize that a social conference is not necessarily interested in the hard-core workshop experience. I have found that many such conferences turn out to be more "reader's conferences", i.e., book buyers, not writers, than a writer's conference. They are fun, especially after spending fifty-one weeks of the year sitting alone at a typewriter or computer, but if party time is not what you're looking for, be wary of the resort conference. However, [he said ambivalently] there can be some very good workshops in such a conference but the chances are they will be jammed. This brings up another point.

Social conferences are usually very large and you can be overwhelmed by the sheer numbers of people there. Then writer's paranoia will immediately assert itself, and you'll think, "I don't belong here," and you may end up spending a week listening silently while your manuscripts mildew in your suitcase. Think about this: every writer there suffers from the same fears, so what you look for are the neurotics; they're probably the writers. I know of one case where a woman arrived at a conference, went to the first cocktail party on the first day, and spent the rest of the week hiding in her room, sneaking out to eat occasionally. [She became a minor character in The Midnight Writers, a novel of mine about writers]

A second type of conference, and much more common, is the academic-intellectual conference, usually held on a college or university campus. If you're not a "serious writer of serious literature," this type of conference could drive you to drink, or whatever other mind-numbing substance you prefer, like watching MTV. The people running such a conference are usually members of the English faculty at the institution, and the writers appearing there are either those currently in favor with the academic-intellectual circles, or friends of the conference directors. Such a conference has a very low tolerance for writers of romance, science fiction, horror, and fantasy. They tolerate the intellectual mystery writer, and they favor minority writing, including feminist fiction, experimental fiction and just about anything out side the mainstream. They are also very partial to poetry. The easiest way to determine the bias of such a conference is to look at its faculty and the writers who are appearing there. The one thing you should have a high tolerance for is the lecture format; this type of conference is about 50% lecture and panel discussions with a Q and A at the end. Also, be prepared for literary interpretation of your writing rather than criticism of the craft of writing. You'll probably hear the word "symbolic" or some form of it, frequently.

There are some writer's conferences held on small college and junior college campuses that are much more oriented toward mainstream writers, that is to say, those in popular fiction. Again, check out the faculty and the writers appearing there. With any conference, read the brochures they send out, very carefully. They tell you, indirectly, what you can expect.

Lately, however, there are a growing number of small writer's conferences, usually sponsored by a writers' group or an individual writer. In once case, I know of a book store owner-writer who established one of the most successful writer's conferences in California, and it's been running now for 17 years. Such a conference can be very valuable for intense workshop experiences and input, but they also carry a danger.

If the conference sponsor is a writer's group, beware of the clique attitude and the protégé syndrome. This can be a very painful experience if you don't fit in or are rejected for some reason, either real or imagined. Writer's groups are very defensive in relation to 'outsiders,' and even though they may have set up the conference, they may still have that 'in group' attitude. I experienced this first hand at a conference in the Sierra where a San Francisco clique of writers dominated it, and it was not much fun. In a large conference you can lose yourself in the crowd, but in a small intimate conference such as these usually are, there is no escape other than leaving it altogether. A second danger lies in the conference sponsored and dominated by an individual writer. It is not uncommon for such a writer to want to turn out writers in his/her own image, and if you resist that kind of criticism, your experience will be negative. To say the least.

The advantage of a good small conference is that you will be on intimate terms with all the writers there and the chance for a very positive experience is much better. There are rarely any "names" there, even though there will probably be published, working writers. If you don't need the thrill of meeting a best selling author or a real New York agent or editor, and you are basically concerned about your writing, then this type of conference may offer the most to you.

Every writer's conference has something to offer, most importantly the chance to meet other writers. The whole experience of a conference depends upon your expectations. If you're a little cynical and don't expect miracles, such as an editor snatching your manuscript out of your hands and flying immediately back to New York with it, you'll probably survive and may even have fun. The best you can reasonably hope for in any conference is to have some of your work heard and received some valid feedback.

By this time you've no doubt come to the conclusion that attending a writer's conference is akin to playing Russian roulette with five loaded chambers. You're right. But, if you know what you could be faced with before you go, the disappointment won't be as great, and even more importantly you'll know how to make the most out of the experience. If nothing else, it's great raw material for stories.

Let me close on a positive note. To paraphrase Kurt Vonnegut: "Accidental trips are God teaching us to dance."

Tripping the light fantastic, Rose

Setting As Character

I do agree that character and setting are inseparable, one reflects the other constantly, but I think that there are times when setting becomes a character quite apart from being an environment through which a character moves and reacts to, and which influences them. Faulkner, Welty, O'Conner, Cormac McCarthy, Steinbeck all seem to see setting as character. It's interesting that the most dominant group of writers who do see setting this way, are from the South. It's fairly clear in their writing, especially in novels such as McCarthy's *Suttree* or *Blood Meridian.* Raymond Chandler made L.A. a character in his mysteries as does James Lee Burke.

There are times in all these writer's works when the setting seems to separate from the character and take on a personality of its own. London was probably the most socio-political user of this idea. I'm interested in speculating why some writers use setting this way and why others simply see setting as the stage upon which their characters play out their lives. In my own experience, I've found that writers from the West have a different concept of space than those from the East, and those from a rural background are different in their conception of environment as a separate entity, than the urban or suburban writer.

I've found in my own writing that setting, or a sense of place, is probably equal in importance to characterization. In thinking of why that is the case, it seems to me to be my reaction to the rootlessness of

America in general, which explains to me our need to find the familiar when we're on the move. The need is expressed through fast food franchises, shopping malls, suburban developments, all of which substitute a superficial similarity with each other for actual place. To me, suburban America seems to be all surface. My characters also react to these things directly and indirectly. For example, when a character notices great sensory details of a particular place, s/he is not only saying "This place matters to me," s/he is also saying to the reader, pay attention, this is significant. Any time I have a character relate the setting to the reader, I'm placing extraordinary stress on it. In the distant voice, I'm stressing it, but in a more removed manner, a more considered thought process. Maybe even philosophic. God forbid.

Adding Words To Our Online Vocabulary

One of the writers on the Art and Integrity in Fiction board suggested these two words to give a quick reaction to a post. "Grrrrr" indicated serious disagreement, possibly anger, and "Hmmmmm:" indicated an interested reaction, as in, let me think about that.

To those two, let me add: "Er, ah:" I'm totally nonplussed, at a loss for words, possibly even thoughts

"Listen listen:" I, on the other hand, am plussed.

(note:"plussed" comes from the Society for the Lost Positive. For example if one can be disgruntled, why not gruntled?)

"Whut?" I'm about to take offense unless what you said is clarified.

"Whut!" I have now taken offense.

"Thumpity, thumpity:" I am beating my breast with guilt and remorse, aka mea culpa.

"Sigh:" I wish I'd said that.

"Siiiigh-thumpity:" I wish I hadn't said that.

"Sniff:" I disagree, to a degree.

"Aarrrrrgh:" I disagree to a great degree. (combines with grrrrr for even more emphasis)

"Snort:" we shouldn't be laughing, but...

"I – Beg – your – pardon:" reserved offense taken at this point, please clarify.

I – beg – your – Pardon!: your clarification substantiated the original offense taken.

(note: both the "I begs" and the "Whuts" say essentially the same thing, however the 'whuts' are more Snopsesian in their utterance, while the 'I begs' are clearly Noel Cowardish. The choice of their use depends upon the level of discussion, i.e., white trash vs effete)

"Really?:" I don't believe this for a minute. (combines with hmmm, as in hmmmm,really?)

"Yeahbut:" You've misunderstood me.

"Reaaaaly? I don't think so."

Well, it can go on forever, but that, my dears, is the beauty of language.

I remain, ever gruntled, Rose

Several Reasons For Keeping An Author Silent During A Critique

[Q: the question came up in relation to my Asilomar Workshop Method in which the writer is not allowed to say anything during the critique session.]

Very, very interesting, and on many points I am in complete agreement with you but I think we differ in what we want the ultimate impact of our workshops to be.

Something I need to point out; I'm talking about a workshop in which the material is read to the group, not one in which we have the manuscript before the workshop and everyone has read it and made notes on it. The read and critique workshop is the most difficult form to run and to run successfully, so ground rules are absolutely necessary. I think you can also see why a conversation between the writer and anyone else during the critique session is very iffy given this type of workshop. In the workshops I run I'm trying to teach one of the most difficult things for anyone to learn; how to listen. And for writers, that is nearly impossible.

I think one thing has been misunderstood about not letting the writer speak until the end of the critique. I meant that there would be no one else in the workshop directly asking questions of the writer during the critique session and that the writer was not allowed to interrupt any critic. If you allow that, "Mere anarchy is loosed upon the world," and the workshop can degenerate into an ugly shouting match or a pointless debating society with everyone either taking sides or sitting quietly, deciding to never, ever do this workshop thing again.

However, I am ambivalent about the workshop leader and writer engaging in conversation for several reasons.

I don't agree that without conversations between the workshop leader and the writer about the manuscript, the focus will be only on the success of this particular manuscript. In any case, the workshop assumes that the manuscript being critiqued is a manuscript that the author feels needs more work. If the attitude of the workshop is that you bring only pieces that you consider to be finished pieces, then there is no point to a critique; all there should be is applause or suggestions of how to rewrite it in order to 'make it stronger or more powerful', which I also believe is not the business of a workshop. Rewriting in a critique is one of the things I ban in my workshop. The writer must make that decision based upon objective criticism of the craft.

For example, if a writer has a minor character who appears in a chapter or scene and that character demands more development and a larger role than the writer has given him/her, the critique would say something about the technique of letting a minor character dominate a major character, or something like that. In other words, it would be a technique or craft point being made. After that it's up to the writer to decide whether or not to change the story so the minor character becomes major or secondary, but it is not the business of the workshop or the workshop leader to say that. It's also up to the writer to interpret the criticism, to think about what it really means in terms of what he/she intended to do, and then they rewrite. To tell them what needs to be rewritten is making them too dependent upon input and not upon their own critical evaluation of the input or upon their own critical eye.

Speaking of writer's intentions, in my experience, most discussions between the writer and anyone else in the workshop, usually end up with the writer saying, "But I intended..." and then it goes on from there, usually badly. A writer's intentions should be evident in the story, and they can't really be critiqued. Intentions fail in the craft of writing, and that's what should be discussed.

In my mind I am trying to give each writer in the workshop insight into their writing, but of equal importance, insight into their own critical eye. This is tricky. In my workshops when a writer's work is being considered, I think the people critiquing are getting as much as the writer, possibly more, because they're more objective about someone else's writing and they can hear criticism more clearly. This tends to put a lot pressure on each individual to be totally participating, all the time, which is why these workshops tend to be very intense. And very valuable. The pressure also eliminates the prima donnas very rapidly, as well as the hobbyists.

The writer under consideration is putting her/his ego on the line, their art, and I know that is a subjective thing to go through no matter how long you've been doing it. And when the writer responds to a workshop leader's questions, their reactions range from defensive to aggressive to compliant; all subjective reactions. The writer being critiqued usually isn't thinking that clearly at that moment, and so responses to questions under duress are, more often that not, emotional rather than logical. And being critiqued by a group is definitely being 'under duress,' no matter how friendly the workshop atmosphere is, and no matter how many times you've done it.

I lay the ground rules of the workshop out very carefully, all of them geared toward one basic concept: respect for each other, including the one about the writer not speaking until the end of all critiques, including the workshop leader's. I find that if I do interrupt the critiques to ask for clarification, etc (and I did do this at one time), I compromise the rest of the critiques in the workshop in that they will either take my lead and focus there, or they will deliberately contradict, or they will feel hesitant to bring something up I didn't focus on. This is more the case in workshops I've just started or at a writer's conference where I know no one.

There is an attitude in workshops among the people participating, that encourages them to follow the workshop leader's lead; after all, the workshop leader is the 'resident authority,' so to follow is to emulate the 'one who knows.' This is particularly a problem with new writers, and even more a problem with young writers. That's why I back off. I suppose I'm using the velvet hammer technique here, but I'm trying to 'empower' them as writers. (sorry for that use of a catch word but it does express here what I'm trying to do)

In order to compensate for the silence of the writer, I ask the writer being critiqued to make notes on their manuscript of comments that they didn't understand, or which they felt 'missed the point,' etc. and at the end of my critique and summary, I throw open the discussion to everyone, writer and critics alike, and I more or less back off and let them go. That's when a lot of very valuable exchanges take place, but before that can happen there has to be a group attitude of respect and concern established. I usually try to have one or two people in a workshop that have worked with me before, so I let them be the models for the group, to see and hear how a critique is given, which establishes the group attitude so that the general open session at the end keeps the workshop atmosphere of mutual respect rather than hostile argumentation. When I do find myself in a workshop in which I know no one, my attitude is the most critical thing in establishing a creative atmosphere, and the one thing I stress and try to project, is respect for everyone in the workshop.

I think one of the most critical things I do as a workshop leader is the summary of the group's critiques. It's here I focus the workshop's comments so that the writer can hear these comments through one voice, mine. I omit the trivial, the obviously mistaken, etc. They know I have no agenda other than to help them with their writing, so any comments from someone else that may have hurt before, are given an objective tone through me and the writer can see it a little more clearly. It also helps that they're hearing a comment or comments for a second time. I take the salient points that have been made, re-emphasize them and point out that I agree and why, (which gives the critic more confidence in his/her own eye), and mention those points that I have missed but which someone else picked up and are critical. And I always give credit to the individual critics. One thing I do not do is directly disagree (by name) with any criticism and I encourage everyone else to not do that. You disagree by contradicting the criticism, not the critic. That keeps it objective rather than personal. However, I do mention names when agreeing with a criticism, because that is positive feedback for the critic. I try to emphasize through the summary that we are pooling our insights, and it's not a single critical eye at work here, it's all of us.

My attitude in the workshop is that I'm working with all of them, all the time, not just one writer at a time. I want to create that unified attitude in the workshop and in the critiquing, and at the same time, encourage individual expression in the writing.

Basically, what I'm saying to them is that there are communal standards of excellence in writing that we all know, some consciously, some unconsciously, and in the workshop I want everyone to become conscious of those standards. Your choice of subject, your genre, etc. is irrelevant. What we discuss is the craft, the techniques of fiction. Experimentation is fine if it doesn't violate a basic rule: don't accidentally confuse the reader.

I have strong reservations about a writer explaining to me or to the group, what they intended to do. I absolutely believe you can talk your story to death, and you can discuss it to death. What a writer needs to do, is take what has been said into their mind and deal with it later, at home on the rewrite. However, if I were in a one on one situation with the writer, then we would have a conversation about the piece and I would be teaching an individual rather than a group. I think that's the basic difference, the individual versus the group approach.

For new writers and young writers the ability to explain the story off the page is not, in my mind, a good habit to get into during the formal critique session. I think if they come to realize that they are committed to what is on the page, even temporarily, there will be more care taken in putting it down. Giving a writer a chance to explain what they meant does not, in my mind, encourage preciseness of language, and rewriting before they make it public, even for the first time, even for a workshop. It needs to be clear to everyone, that reading in a workshop is not that they're taking their last, best shot; this is the first public shot and they need feedback to see if it's doing what they intended it to do. Any piece read should be as good as the writer can make it, but if they think it's finished, it shouldn't be read because all that will happen is they will be hurt or offended.

Too often I see in workshops, people offering something that they haven't really worked on much, a first, very rough draft. I hear them say, "Well, this is just something I dashed off last night." There's probably a reason for that. They can kid themselves or everyone else, that they didn't really try that hard; it's just a first rough draft. That to me is a large load of crap. I always tell my workshops to show some care, some seriousness about writing, and the group will take you seriously.

In the informal session at the end, it helps everyone primarily because I've removed myself as the authority figure which more or less means this discussion is among writers about writing in general, not a specific consideration of this specific piece. I am also called to task there, clarifying a point, expanding on another, and that's where the best teaching comes in for the individual and the group. It's there that I establish the peer quality of the group, i.e., we are all writers and I can be challenged or questioned too. Often I find myself discussing the piece with the writer, discussing the points I brought up during the critique session.

The conversation about the work comes at the end, not during the critique session. This puts an incredible amount of pressure on the workshop leader, and it should. You've got to be absolutely involved in every critique so that the summary will be clear and focused and take the best of what was offered.

I think a conversation between the writer and the workshop leader during the formal session, is too exclusionary, and indirectly tells the group that this part of the session is for the benefit of this writer only. In my mind that is not the purpose of a workshop. And I think allowing the author to interrupt a critic is suicidal. I am again reminded of Yeats : "Things fall apart; the centre cannot hold…The blood dimmed tide is loosed…" I think that is the death of a workshop, primarily because it becomes a debating society at best. At worst, who knows? Sharks in a feeding frenzy comes to mind.

One thing I ask critics to not do in the critique session is line edit. Any grammar glitches, etc. can be written down and given to the writer later, but that is not the focus of the workshop. I've also noticed that the 'damning with faint praise' or focusing on the trivial may happen once, with a new member of the group, but they quickly understand that this workshop doesn't do that, particularly when they see that I ignore those remarks in my summary. There is a seriousness, and a camaraderie, that permeates the group which quickly discourages inane criticism.

Now, given all that, I am also convinced that each of us run our workshops according to our own personalities and teaching styles. What works for one won't work for another. I've been told that I have an overwhelming, dominating, almost intimidating style in the workshop and/or classroom because I am "overly enthusiastic." [god forbid anyone should have passion about anything] Hence, I have to consciously back off and give more apparent control to the group, even though I'm orchestrating it very carefully.

But sometimes I feel as if I'm trying to organize a cloud of gnats. Sometimes I long for a cloud of gnats!

My best to you,
Rose

Curing Not Snubbing

[Q: In our writer's group we seem to have problems with the romance writers refusal to deviate from the basic formula. How do you cure them of this?]

The point is, as I think Roy makes in one of his posts, that these romance writers do not want to be cured. They want to be reassured that they are 'writers' and when they don't get that reassurance, they simply ignore the message, which is probably the critiques that call the basic formula into question.

This, I think, is also tied to the teaching of writing in all its forms, from basic composition to poetry, i.e., students beyond the sixth grade don't want to be told they don't know how to write or that their writing skills are at a very basic level. Romance writers that I've seen in my workshops, have been very uncertain, and sometimes even apologetic, about their genre, which is not very positive. The thing is, if a writer goes into a workshop, that isn't specifically focused on the romance genre, they're laying themselves open to serious problems. It's difficult to discuss something like characterization, if the genre demands two dimensional characterization. The same applies to setting, plot lines, dialog, etcetera. When a writer decides to become a formula writer, all they should care about is if they are applying the formula well. This means they belong in a romance genre workshop, not a general writing workshop.

Another aspect of the problem is who is teaching them, usually teachers who do not specialize in writing and who in fact write just adequately themselves. At the university level, the teaching of writing is usually done by part timers, who in fact may be the best choice to teach writing because the tenured faculty are specialists in the reading and analysis of literature, not writing. Most of the teachers in my university, look on the teaching of writing classes either as punishment, a distasteful duty they must occasionally accept. Teaching creative writing, however, is looked upon as being time off, a reward for teaching lit classes, a 'fun' class.

There are also too many of the 'touchy-feely' teachers in creative writing who seem to think that simply making their students feel good about their writing is their purpose. A close examination usually shows that they don't really know the craft of writing that well, they write more from instinct and feeling, which is okay but not if you're teaching writing. In the university I taught in, there was a professor who read his poetry to his creative writing class, and cried as he read. I don't know what he thought he was establishing there, but I found it ludicrous and too much of an ego trip to be a valid approach to teaching. His focus was on his needs, not the needs of the students.

There are very few writers out here who truly love writing, who can also teach it. That combination is very, very rare and when you do find an actual teaching-writer, if they have any kind of name at all, the writing workshops are compromised by that fame. For example, what student would dare ask a famous writer for clarification of a critical remark. And too many times, the students try to imitate the success of the writer-teacher rather than develop their own styles. Most of the famous writers that I've met are great at lectures but lousy at teaching. Face it; you have to be very selfish to be a writer.

To return to my original point about curing not snubbing; I've accepted the fact that in running workshops and teaching classes, the discovery of a true writer is a rare occasion, but one that makes everything worth it. So far, in 12 years of university teaching I've only run across perhaps a dozen real writers. In the workshops outside the university I've seen quite a few more because the screening process is much more 'brutal.' People take themselves out of the workshops. No one tells them to leave, but the level of writing and criticism is so high it requires very serious work that they either don't want to involve themselves in or they realize is beyond them.

You cannot teach the love of writing, the obsession with the written word, the joy of realizing you have, at some point, accomplished what you wanted, even if it is only a single passage in a novel. If an individual doesn't have that love, there is no hope for them as writers. I don't snub them, and unfortunately there is no cure for that.

A final word: just recently a former student from 1967, tracked me down on the internet, and then called me. We talked for about an hour, during which time he told me he was still writing, and he e-mailed me some of his work. That was a great feeling.

Bashing Vs. Venting

[Q: when we're arguing here [Art and Integrity in Fiction board] are we really bashing each other?]

I think what we're doing here is venting, not bashing, but passionate venting does frighten people. It's odd in a way, but so far I don't see anyone trying to convince anyone else of anything, which is also good. We're in the area of intellectual exchange.

I noticed that there seems to be a sharing of anger, sometimes even rage, but I prefer to keep my rage intact to use in my writing. This board provides a vent so the pressure building in me doesn't explode destructively. I think we're all very careful here to not let that happen because there is a real feeling of respect for the people on the board. It's very clear that we don't want to be misunderstood and we don't want to attack each other.

Rage is best expressed on the written page where it can be shaped, honed, worked until it ceases being a great, clumsy club and becomes a laser able to cut through the ugliness of society that enrages us. If we're really good, it can make a difference, and even if that doesn't happen, we've done something that I think embodies the highest purpose of human beings; we've channeled a destructive urge into a creative process.

I like the way this board keeps us honest by never letting a careless or thoughtless comment that could be misunderstood, get by. Great reminders for those of us who say exactly what we mean after we've said exactly what we felt, also known as the engage brain before operating mouth rule. I am always impressed by the preciseness of language we encourage each other to use.

I think it was AD who said here at one point that he was relieved that we weren't exchanging plots, story lines, works in progress reports, asking for feedback. (see AD, you are quotable, albeit indirectly and loosely) I too am thankful for that…to talk about anything I'm writing or intend to write dissipates the passion of it. This board tends to focus or clarify that passion because we're dealing with the art and integrity of writing not our writing.

I wonder if anyone else finds the short story as the ideal form for rage, and the novel as the better form for sustained anger. I've even gone into poetry to express some of my most intense feelings of rage. Anybody else looking at the forms that way?

The Workshop

Workshops are something dear to my heart so I must say this. I've been running workshops for over 30 years either through a conference, a university or just out in the world of reality. I started a workshop 27 years ago and it is still going strong. The southern California branch meets every two weeks and I do not know how they can manage it that frequently. They've told me it's addictive. The northern California branch meets every four or five weeks. Twice a year,once in January and once in July we meet at the Asilomar State Park near Monterey and read and critique for three days and three nights. We have a publishing record that is phenomenal and we are constantly bringing in new talent.

This workshop works for one reason; we all base our critiques on this philosophy: "How can I help make it better." Not what can I find wrong, which is destructive. We all know that we could read Tolstoy and find something wrong, but could any of us make it better? This not only helps focus the critiquing it helps the writer whose work is under consideration understand what the group is doing; they're trying to help.

We also have one basic aim in a workshop: to put the writer in control of her/his writing. That's why we address craft only.

In my mind there are several things about a workshop that are critical, and the most critical is having someone run it. I don't believe that democracy works in a workshop. What usually happens is a series of debates or arguments among the critics while the writer sits there. Someone has to keep the group focused on the job at hand and the job is giving the writer a thoughtful and clear critique. The person running the workshop clearly has to have the respect of the group.

We have several basic rules in the workshop, among them, the writer may say nothing to anyone until all critiques are finished. This prevents endless explanations or arguments. Our point here is, "If it's not on the page, it doesn't exist." We also allow no critiques of critiques. Everyone must address their comments to the writer and no one else. The workshop leader critiques last and gives a summary of the major points the group has made. You can readily see that being the workshop leader is not an easy task.

The value of a workshop to new or young writers is that it gives them a vocabulary for things they are doing without knowing they're doing it. Most beginning writers of any age write from instinct, usually a result of a serious reading habit. That's fine, but unless they know how they are using those techniques they simply absorbed they will never be in control of their writing. That goes for experienced, published professionals as well. You can always gain more control over your writing.

We also tell everyone who is new to the workshop to not bring something you feel is a finished product. We are not meeting for applause and mutual admiration. We bring pieces to the workshop that we have doubts about, or that are new and we're just feeling our way with them, or ones we know aren't working but we can't figure out why, etc. etc. That way, when you get critiqued you don't feel as if you're being assaulted, you're being helped.

I am very suspicious of most university workshops. They seem to me to be either "My, aren't we all wonderfully creative" groups, or shark feeding frenzies or run by academic writers who are more interested in turning out a recognizable product than an individual writer. They are also terrible genre snobs. I had a young woman in my university workshop who writes beautiful sword and sorcerer novels, she is very, very talented, but she was ridiculed by some of the professorial types for her choice of genre. That's another thing about our workshop; we don't care what you're writing as long as it's the best that you can write in that field. We have no gender, no race. We're just writers.

Mentoring

[Q: What do you think about writers serving as mentors for new writers?]

I have to agree with John G. having gone through exactly the same experiences with beginning writers. Our problem as 'mentors' is that it's impossible to quickly sort out the poseurs from the serious. The easiest way is also the most difficult, i.e., you must see the manuscript. If it comes in full of errors, poorly typed or, god forbid, handwritten, etc. it indicates someone who has no pride in their medium. I won't even consider them. After that, in my mind it depends more upon how they take criticism, that is, do they listen and then try to rewrite. It seems to me if someone asks me to critique a story or novel, they're doing so because they respect my judgment for some reason, usually word of mouth. If they don't like what they get, okay, but don't attack me because you don't want to believe it or you doubt me. Go on and do it yourself.

One of the worst kinds I've run across is the "success by attrition" writer, the one who gives you a story, you critique it, they "rewrite" it, give it back to you and there are no serious changes, so you give it back, and it comes back again and again and again in the same form. The hope is you'll finally give in. For me, after the first time, I won't look at it again, but I've been put in situations in writer's conferences where this happens. In one instance a writer of zero talent, which was perfected over three years into less than zero talent, was finally give an award by the conference directors just to get this person out of their hair. Mistake. This same individual is now offering services as a 'workshop facilitator.' Jesus. This person has the critical insight of a speed bump. It occurred to me then, to send all these poseurs to this person's workshop. A level of hell I can't even imagine. And such poetic justice it "makes me gleeful."

About extremely successful writers "owing something" to the art or craft. I don't think they do. Their writing is their 'payment' of debt. They are perfecting the craft, hopefully, and we can look to them as models. To give direct help, well, that goes on all the time. Look at the book blurbs. I've had successful writers recommend me to agents and publishers but only after they knew me personally for quite some time. It's not something you do casually. When a writer does recommend someone, they are putting their name on the line as well, an endorsement not to be taken lightly and not to be given lightly. I can't imagine Bill Styron or Annie Proulx casually recommending anyone to an editor or agent and they shouldn't. I think that's the kind of thing you have to earn. It's not owed to you. Of course then you have the professional blurb writers such as Clive Cussler.

Audience

[Q: "Am I writing for you or for me?" This question came up when a submission to a board on AOL was rejected because it used "offensive language."]

An interesting, albeit ambivalent, rhetorical question, i.e., I have no idea how you would answer but it set me off thinking about the idea of audience and the vehicle through which you're going to reach that audience.

My first assumption is that when you decide to write for reasons other than a hobby or therapy, your aim is to reach an audience. You are not writing for yourself. You are writing for an audience. Anything that gets in the way of reaching that audience has to be considered very carefully and dealt with. In this particular case, you knew what the restrictions of AOL were, but also felt the integrity of what you were writing demanded that you ignore AOL's editorial policy and go ahead and post your story the way you wrote it. Why are you surprised? Why are you outraged? This isn't necessarily a violation of the First Amendment, but it is a violation of considered submission to a publisher who would be more open to what you're doing.

It's the same anywhere else you submit for publication. For example you don't use the "mf" word if you're submitting to Good Housekeeping. If you think that's where your audience is, you have to find a replacement for "mf." If you can't and the integrity of the piece is compromised to the point that it no longer works, then forget *Good Housekeeping.*

This doesn't mean that you shape everything you write to fit a particular publication or publisher. You write what you feel you have to, then you have to take into consideration where it stands the best chance of acceptance. You look for those outlets that are compatible with your world view, etc. When you make a mistake, as you apparently did here, your reaction should be Ah Ha! Now I know what they're all about, and you flee to the nearest exit, clutching your work to your bosom before it is mediocritized to death. (how's that for a new literary verb?)

Given all that, I do have to agree that AOL standards or guidelines seem a little strange given the complex and varied nature of the 'audience'. It looks like AOL is striving to hit the middle ground of morality, that is we will offend no one in case the kids are lurking. I agree that this is ridiculous and results in arbitrary censorship so people suffering through childhood, puberty and/or adolescence won't be offended, or warped, or, much more likely, their parents won't be offended. Clearly they're already warped.

So, RT, consider the situation you put yourself in and laugh it off. Then submit your piece in a forum that will judge it on its merit rather than on its use of 'offensive language.'

Submittingly yours, Rose

Humor And Satire

It sounds like your friend misunderstood the authorial stance in good satire which I think is the ability to see the absurdity of the situation and be able to laugh at it as well as despise it. Simple hatred is a raw emotion and so unfunny that it is ineffective as satire. A literary attack based on hatred, demands a different technique, perhaps expose, but certainly not humor or satire. Another problem with hatred is that the reader must share the depth of emotion the author feels, and that is not often the case.

I think Annie Proulx uses a very subtle form of humor in her latest book *Accordion Crimes*, for example the selection of the accordion itself as the unifying device of the book. There are a few instruments that might be taken less seriously, for example toilet paper and a comb, the kazoo, or a tuba, but when you think about her audience, and I believe she is writing to an intellectual audience, or at least a pseudo intellectual audience, to select the accordion as the unifying element of the episodes is humorous. Some people think the accordion itself is a musical crime…among my jazz aficionado friends there is a bumper sticker that reads: *Use An Accordion, Go To Jail.*

Also in the same book she uses juxtaposition in an unusual way. After describing a particularly depressing scene in a hospital emergency room, she ends the entire episode with this line: “And the room smelled of guinea pigs,” a propos of nothing! You can’t help laughing out loud. I think that may also be comic relief.

I wrote a story entitled *The Night The Colonel Killed Doris Day,* which was satire and broad humor mixed with a little slapstick. My intention was to satirize right wing militarists, cheap roadside attractions and American poor taste in what entertains us. Let me emphasize that one pronoun…us…because for it to be funny I had to also be a part of that poor taste. I had to be able to laugh at myself before I could expect anyone else to laugh. An editor read it, loved and sent me a note saying that the story “…makes me gleeful.” That is the exact reaction I wanted, glee, that happy laughter when you see something ridiculous that is being taken seriously, suddenly exploded.

And if I may take a chance and mention Woody Allen; his self deprecating humor is very effective because he is asking us to laugh with him, at his persona as a representative of our own pretensions, etc.

For example, aggressive American patriotism is satirized when Allen says he has a new draft classification: in case of war he is a hostage, which goes with his overall comic persona as a non aggressive, ineffective uber nerd.

laughingly yours, Rose

The Creativity In Outlining

[Q: How do you contrive an outline for a story?]

Well, an outline is not exactly contriving. You put your character, whom you must know intimately, in a given situation, in a given place and time, and your character reacts as she/he must react given their personalities, etc. You, as the creator of this character, must have a reason for observing this character in this situation other than just chasing along after them to see what they do. Chasing them with a notebook may be fun and it may feel creative, but it ain't. I think you have to give your characters a world with boundaries and let them move within those boundaries. The creative part is when you discover that your character, and the personality you've given her/him, pushes those boundaries further than you thought they would or could, because in the writing you discovered new possibilities in them. That's why story is character. The plot doesn't alter all that much, but getting from the beginning to the end does.

Let me draw an analogy: when I plot out a novel I put myself in the position of being a God who believes she/he is omnipotent and omniscient, and I create a world for these characters that is realistic, believable and looks predictable. Then I make a deliberately creative mistake: I create a character who is not only believable, but in this world of fiction that I'm creating, I intensify the character and, here's the mistake; I give the character free will. That's where the character does things that I didn't expect but could have predicted if I had paid more attention to the qualities I endowed her/him with. That's where the exciting part of writing comes in. And even though I know the character is going to win or lose, I don't know exactly how they're going to arrive at that point and what they're going to learn about themselves and life in general along the way. That's also the God of fiction's learning process.

I have to know, generally, how the story is going to end. It is critical in giving the story meaning, and in giving the plot a drive it wouldn't ordinarily have. That is called narrative pull, and what that adds to the story for the reader, is a sense of inevitability, the feeling that, yes, that had to happen because of who the character is. It doesn't necessarily mean that the reader knows what's going to happen, but they have this feeling of the character being inexorably drawn toward their fate, which means they believe in the world you've created and when they get to the climax they know it had to happen this way.

Why do I get the feeling that I've just chipped out some commandments in stone?

Well, trust God. She can change Her mind.

Prophetically yours, Rose

BASICS OF WRITING FICTION OR THE COMMANDMENTS

FICTION IS INTENSIFIED REALITY
CHARACTER IS STORY
Five types of characters:
Central: your main character through which everything is focused
Secondary: important, but only in relation to central character; some development of character
Minor: named, with some identifying traits, speaking
Background: only there for reality, like shrubs, trees, etc.
Catalyst: can be anyone but the central character. Frequently is an absent character, one never seen, or a walk on.
In a mystery the corpse can be the catalyst

SHOW DON'T TELL (some exceptions)
4 POINT PLOT FORMULA:
CONFLICT (what drives the story, not necessarily man vs_man)
COMPLICATION (although these are helpful) man vs self
CRISIS man vs the divine
CONCLUSION man vs nature

POINT OF VIEW [each p.o.v. here has two voices, close and distant]

FIRST: a story of character, has limitations limited due to single focus p.o.v. that works well with present tense. close voice here is the voice of the narrator at the time of the story; distant voice here is the voice of the narrator recalling the story

THIRD: most common, no limitations (a danger), usually past tense used different type of tension, i.e., you know the narrator, close voice here is the voice of the character, distant voice here is the voice of the narrator, outside the story

BEGINNINGS:

Generalization: My mother believed you could be anything you wanted to be in America. (Amy Tan, *Two Kinds*)

Description of a person: He was lifting his knees high and putting his hand up, when I first saw him, as if crossing the road through that stringing rain, he were breaking through the bead curtain of a Pernambuco bar.(V.S. Pritchett, *The Sailor*]

Narrative summary: The strange thing was, he said, how they screamed every night at midnight. I do not know why they screamed at that time. [Hemingway, *On The Quai at Smyrna*]

With Dialogue: "Don't think about a cow," Matt Brinkley said. (Anne Beattie)

With several characters, but no dialogue: When they came south out of Grant County, Boyd was not much more than a baby and the newly formed county they'd named Hidalgo was itself little older than the child. In the country they'd quit lay the bones of a sister and the bones of his maternal grandmother. [Cormac McCarthy, *The Crossing*]

With a Setting and only One Character: Old Dudley folded into the chair he was gradually molding to his own shape and looked out the window fifteen feet away into another window framed by blackened red brick. He was waiting for the geranium. They put it out every morning about ten and they took it in at five-thirty. [Flannery O'Connor, *The Geranium*]

With A Reminiscent Narrator: I know what they said. They said I didn't run away from home but that I was tolled away by a crazy man who, if I hadn't killed him first, would have killed me inside another week. [William Faulkner, *Uncle Willy*]

With a Child Narrator: Me and Pete would go down to Old Man Killegrew's and listen to his radio. We would wait until after supper, after dark, and we would stand outside Old Man Killegrew's parlor window, and we could hear it because Old Man Killegrew's wife was deaf, and so he run the radio as loud as it would run, and so me and Pete could hear it plain as Old Man Killegrew's wife could, I reckon, even standing outside with the window closed.[Faulkner, *Two Soldiers*]

By Establishing a Point of View

First Person: "I stand here ironing, and what you asked me moves tormented back and forth with the iron." [Tillie Olsen, *I Stand Here Ironing*]

Third Person,close: He held his breath an instant, dug his nails into the palms of his hands, and said quickly, "I"m in love with you." He saw her redden suddenly, as if someone had slapped her cheeks, which had a smooth and pale sheen to them. [Mario Vargas Llosa, *On Sunday*]

Third Person, distant: Sam Batinovich was on the brink of the Utah-Nevada desert headed into the white hot salt flats. [Carolyn Doty, *A Day Late*]

DIALOGUE:

basic form

function: sounds real but wastes no words, reveals character, provides tension,

moves story forward

business

tags

EXERCISE: write a two person scene in which one character is trying to break through the other character's barrier or denial. Make the issue specific and dramatic. Do it mainly with dialogue but use business to set scene, describe character's expressions, gestures, reactions. Make it a verbal dance.

PLOT EXERCISE: a linear story

Conflict: main character is on a quest for a specific object

no explanation of why the object is needed, ;it's a given

character begins acting immediately

Complication: character meets a specific obstacle

Crisis: obstacle is overwhelming, impossible

Conclusion: character triumphs through magic or supernatural means

SITUATION TO PLOT EXERCISE:

Begin a story using one of the following as your main character:

A person working for a company that is downsizing.

A waitress/waiter who likes to convert sinners on the job.

A person is given a truckload of ducks as payment of a debt.

A commuter who takes an off ramp to avoid a traffic jam.

A retired person buys a Harley Davidson.

Complicate your character's life with opposing forces, tension, conflict

offer the character alternatives

ask what your character wants.

ask what your character would do.

ask how your character would react or act.

write a memory of something that happened to you or a character before the age of seven.

keep the language, etc. consistent with a child of that age.

keep the time span under an hour

keep the setting in one place

there must be a reason for the memory, a "meaning", which is the focus

Objective: to present a narrative without explaining or interpreting the event. A child cannot analyze, but merely tell the story, without explanations, etc.

tell the same story in the first person adult voice

in the first person, write a self-deceiving portrait in which the narrator is not the person they think they are but the reader keeps getting clues that the narrator is skewing the truth.

THIRD PERSON POINT OF VIEW EXERCISES (500 words max)

Write a third person distant story based on exercise number 3 in the previous exercise, in which the narrator is telling about this self deceiving person.

Write a third person close story based on exercise number 3.

Write a third person distant story in which the omniscient narrator is outside the story and has an attitude but is not part of the story.

PLOTTING EXERCISES (750 words max)

Write a linear story in which a strong main character is on a quest for something important and specific. The object is a given-don't explain its importance. The main character starts acting immediately, meets an obstacle, overcomes it by means of magic or a supernatural element that comes from outside. Tell the story through action and dialogue.

In a few sentences create a specific character in a specific situation. Complicate his/her life with opposing forces and alternatives. (ask what your character wants, what would they do, how would they react and how would their actions propel the story toward a crisis or a final resolution?)

BEGINNING EXERCISE (500 words max)

write an opening for a story that begins with a description of a person

write an opening for a story that begins with a description of a place write an opening for a story that begins with dialogue

write an opening for a story that begins with a third person narrative voice describing the actions of two or more characters.

write an opening for a story that begins with a first person narrator explaining something he/she did

STORY TRIGGERS (550 words)

Certain words can serve as triggers for stories or scenes, one such word is SUNDAY. Write a scene or story based on that trigger.

Compile your own list of at least ten triggers for scenes or stories

VOICE

At a recent meeting of the Asilomar Writer's Consortium, one of the group said that voice and point of view were not the same. I immediately said, they were the same, voice is just a more complex aspect of both first and third person point of view. Voice is the consciousness that relates the story to the reader, and that voice will be either in third distant and close, or first distant and close. The reader's reaction and understanding of the story will depend upon which point of view dominates.

In third person distant p.o.v., you're establishing a voice outside the reality of the fictional world you're creating, thus they do not participate in the events of the novel. This is the voice of truth, the voice the reader can depend upon for total honesty. This voice cannot lie or deceive the reader, as the third person close p.o.v. can. This voice can vary from novel to novel, depending upon what the novel requires. In a sense, it is the voice of the author, but we have to be careful when saying that. If the author's style, attitudes, etcetera, are always the same from novel to novel, then the voice is consistently the same and clearly authorial. Henry James said that the author should get out of the novel and I agree with that for the most part. The voice of each novel fulfills the needs of that novel only. The problem, for me at least, of a recognizable and consistent authorial voice in the third distant point of view, is one of ego. It's the writer saying, "Look at me! Look at me!" instead of letting the characters and the consciousness of the novel dominate, as they should.

The third distant voice does have style and this is evident through the description of settings, characters and events. Any novel is an expression of this third distant voice; the author selected the subject, created the characters, the settings, in fact did everything that is in the book. To constantly step into the book in the persona of the author, indicates an uncertainty about the fictional world being created.

The thing is, the style of the third distant voice has to be clearly different that that of the close voice [character]. If you're following the basic rule of fiction, show don't tell, this means that the third person close voice is going to dominate, so it's the character's style, attitudes, etcetera that come through clearly to the reader, the character's voice. You don't want stylistic confusion between the distant and close voice. The thing here, is that the third distant voice style shouldn't be intrusive or dominating.

FIRST PERSON DISTANT AND CLOSE GRAPHIC

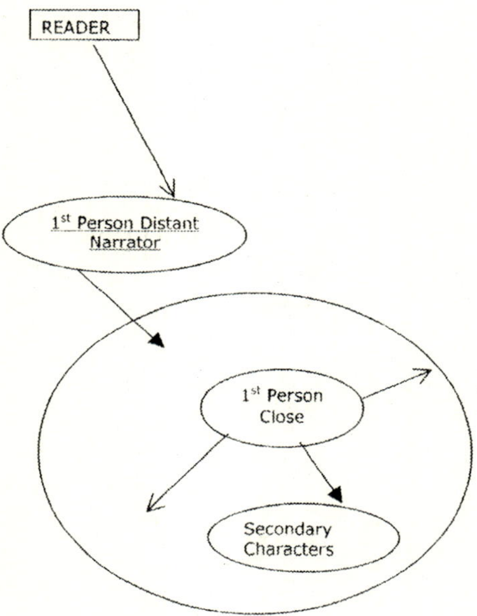

This is a tricky point of view to understand. Here we have a first person narrator, a character, who is telling the reader a story about something that happened in the past. The past can be very recent, like yesterday, or remote, as an adult recalling a childhood experience.

The tricky part is understanding that the 1st person narrator is a character telling the reader a story about an event or events in his/her life. With the opening line of any 1st person story, the reader is immediately in the fictional world. The reader gets no information from any other source.

The thing to remember here is that the distant voice is more a 'telling' voice, and the close voice is a 'showing' voice, so your decision on which voice will dominate will effect the impact of the story on the reader, i.e., the distant voice wants the reader to understand what happened, the close voice wants the reader to share in the emotions of the event. You decide how to 'balance' the two voices.

THIRD PERSON POINT OF VIEW DISTANT GRAPHIC

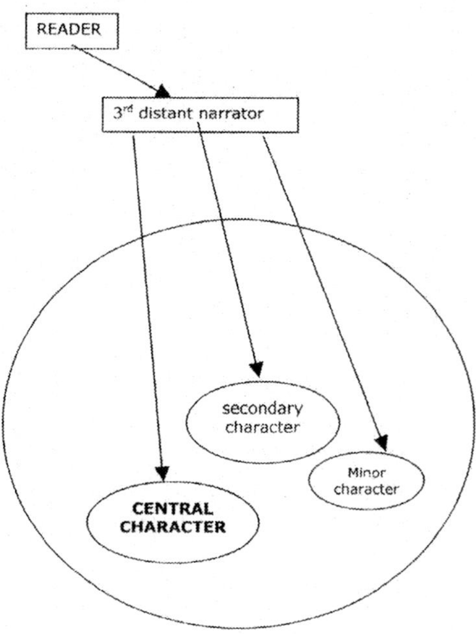

The **3rd distant voice** is always outside the story and tells the reader everything about the story, including the characters. It is not a character.

The 3rd distant voice is the voice of truth in the novel.

Also, the 3rd distant voice can give the reader the thoughts of the other characters as well as of the central character. However if the distant voice goes into the mind of any character, and uses the character's language, it becomes a close voice.

The 3rd distant voice can go into the mind of any character in the story and let the reader view this fictional world through the eyes of whatever character is chosen. This is close voice. Normally, the dominant character within the story is the central character, and the reader sees most of this fictional world through

The distant voice has the ability to go into the mind of any character in the story, thus shifting the point of view from distant to close.

THIRD PERSON CLOSE VOICE GRAPHIC

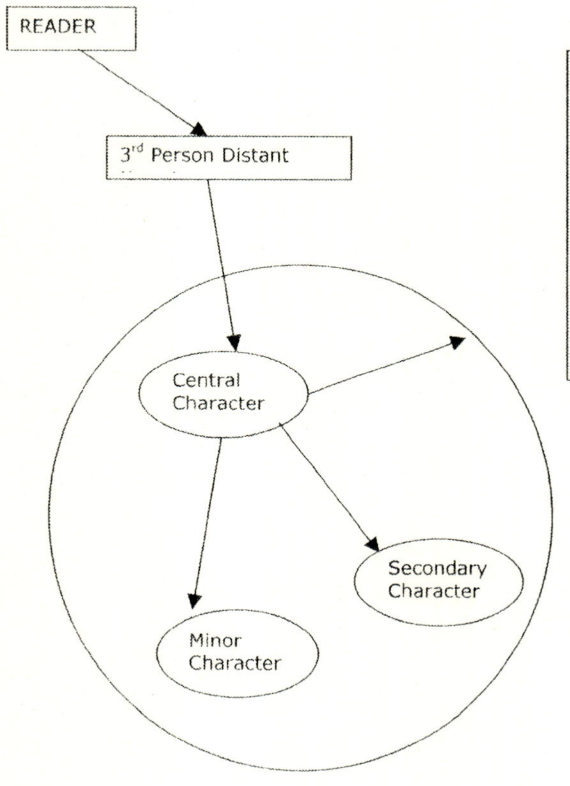

This is the **3rd close point of view.** The reader is taken into the world of the story through the 3rd distant narrator, who then goes into the mind of a central character, and the reader then sees the fictional world through the central character's eyes, and also sees the other characters through the central character's eyes. This is a biased point of view.

THIRD PERSON POV, FOCUS SHIFT GRAPHIC

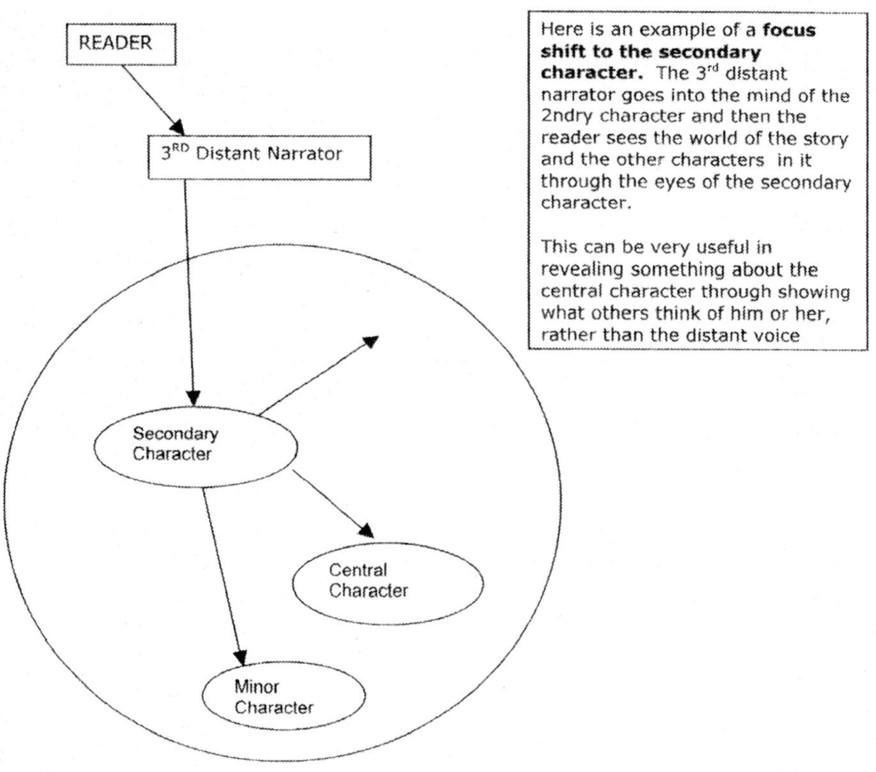

FIRST PERSON POV CLOSE, PRESENT TENSE

GRAPHIC

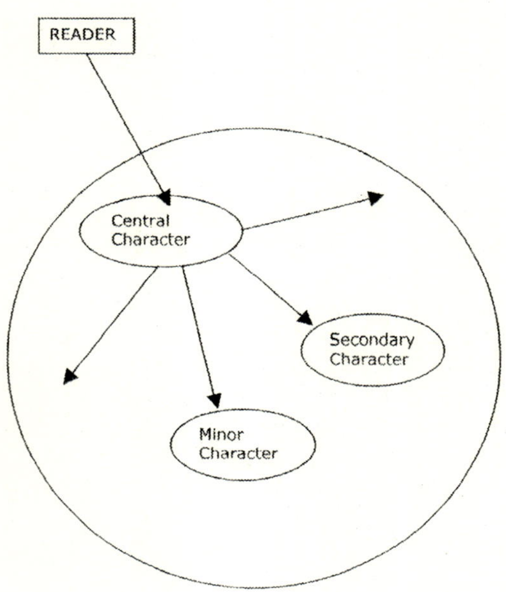

This is a **1st person, close voice story told in present tense**, about an event occurring immediately. This is a difficult point of view to get the reader to accept because the idea of a present tense story is that it is happening as the reader reads it. It's very difficult to get a willing suspension of disbelief with this tense.

Compare this point of view with the 1st person distant, and you'll see immediately that the difference is that the 1st person point of view character is in a fictional world out side the fictional world of the story he or she is telling.

A FINAL WORD

Over the years I've had many discussions about the differences between fiction and non fiction and ultimately it all boils down to one idea for me: non fiction is focused on facts, fiction cares about truth.